Point Pelee
CANADA'S DEEP SOUTH

DARRYL STEWART
WITH CONTRIBUTIONS BY DON ROSS

FOREWORD BY PIERRE BERTON

WAYNE STATE UNIVERSITY PRESS
DETROIT 1977

© 1977 Darryl Stewart

Published in Canada by Burns and MacEachern Limited,
62 Railside Road, Don Mills, Ontario, M3A 1A6.
Published simultaneously in the United States by
Wayne State University Press, Detroit, Michigan 48202.

All rights reserved. No part of this publication
may be reproduced, stored in a retrieval system or
transmitted in any form or by any means, electronic,
mechanical, photocopying, recording or otherwise
without prior written permission.

Drawings by Darryl Stewart

Edited by Jane Lind
Designed by Hugh Michaelson
Printed and bound in Canada by the Alger Press

ISBN 0 88768 073 9

Stewart, Darryl, 1936-
  Point Pelee

Bibliography: p.
ISBN 0-88768-073-9 pa.

1. Natural history — Ontario — Point Pelee
National Park. 2. Point Pelee National Park,
Ont. I. Ross, Don. II. Title.

QH106.2.O5S74   574.9713'31   C77-001318-X

CONTENTS

Foreword by Pierre Berton / 8
Introduction / 11
History of Point Pelee / 17
Major Life Zones / 23
Birds / 33
Mammals / 51
Reptiles and Amphibians / 69
Fish / 81
Insects / 85
Changing Face of Point Pelee / 93
Visiting Point Pelee / 97
A Checklist of Birds / 101
Suggested Reading / 109

ACKNOWLEDGEMENTS
I wish to express my gratitude to the following
 for their cooperation in the writing of this book:
Point Pelee National Park Interpretative Centre
Dr. Ross James, Department of Ornithology,
 Royal Ontario Museum, Toronto
Federation of Ontario Naturalists, Don Mills, Ontario
Ontario Ministry of Natural Resources Research Library,
 Queen's Park Toronto
The Royal Ontario Museum Research Library, Toronto
L. Anne Welwood for her editorial assistance
The late James L. Baillie, Jr. for introducing me to Point Pelee.

To my wife Patricia without whose assistance this book would not have been possible.

Foreword

For more than fifteen years, my wife and I, along with our friends, Fred and Margaret Bodsworth, have made an annual mid-May pilgrimage to Point Pelee to see the birds. There is no annual ritual — not even Christmas — to which I look forward with greater anticipation. For Pelee in May, — when the leaves are about to burst from the trees, when the Sweet Cicely and the Herb Robert carpet the ground, when the Redbud is aflame, when the marshes echo with the chatter of the redwings and the foliage is spangled by the butterfly hues of the wood warblers — Pelee in May is as close as I wish to be to paradise.

We rise with the horned larks and head out in the slightly chilly dawn to the Point to view the gulls and the terns and those accidental birds who, having come too far, flit, bewildered, from sassafras to shagbark, wondering where in hell they are. On my very first visit to Pelee I saw my first rarity, a baffled Le Conte's sparrow, who remained frozen to a single grassy clump for the entire weekend. And sometimes at the Point, as the early sun begins to warm the sands, we are lucky enough to find ourselves in the midst of a migrating wave swooping across Lake Erie on a warm front — thousands of white-crowned sparrows, perhaps, or trees alive with goldfinch and siskin.

And so we make our way slowly back, through the woods into the orchard, along the nature trail, across the marsh, and along the sand dunes where the hoary puccoon grows. Pelee is all things to all nature lovers: there is an environment for every bird it seems, and there are shrubs and flowers here that grow nowhere else in Canada.

There is also the camaraderie of Pelee, especially on the two big birding weekends in May. Here one meets new friends and encounters old ones. Utter strangers will rush up to inform you that a blue grosbeak has been spotted near the orchard or that a dickcissel has been positively identified on the nature trail. We brim over with gratitude and rush off to spot the rarity. Later, if we can, we return the favour.

For Pelee is more than birds. For me it is the ultimate rite of spring. It is the perfume of the spice bush, the sound of bacon sizzling, the taste of wild asparagus, the buzzing of the woodcock, the pungency of barbecued steak, or the spectacle of a dozen Blackburnian warblers, orange against the new green of spring. Pelee is more than a national park; it is a celebration. I write these words in mid-April, after one of the coldest winters on record. The snow has only recently fled and, if my nature diary is any indication, we will have one more flurry yet before spring can properly be said to have arrived. Once again Pelee beckons and I can hardly wait to answer the call.

PIERRE BERTON
KLEINBURG, ONTARIO
APRIL, 1977

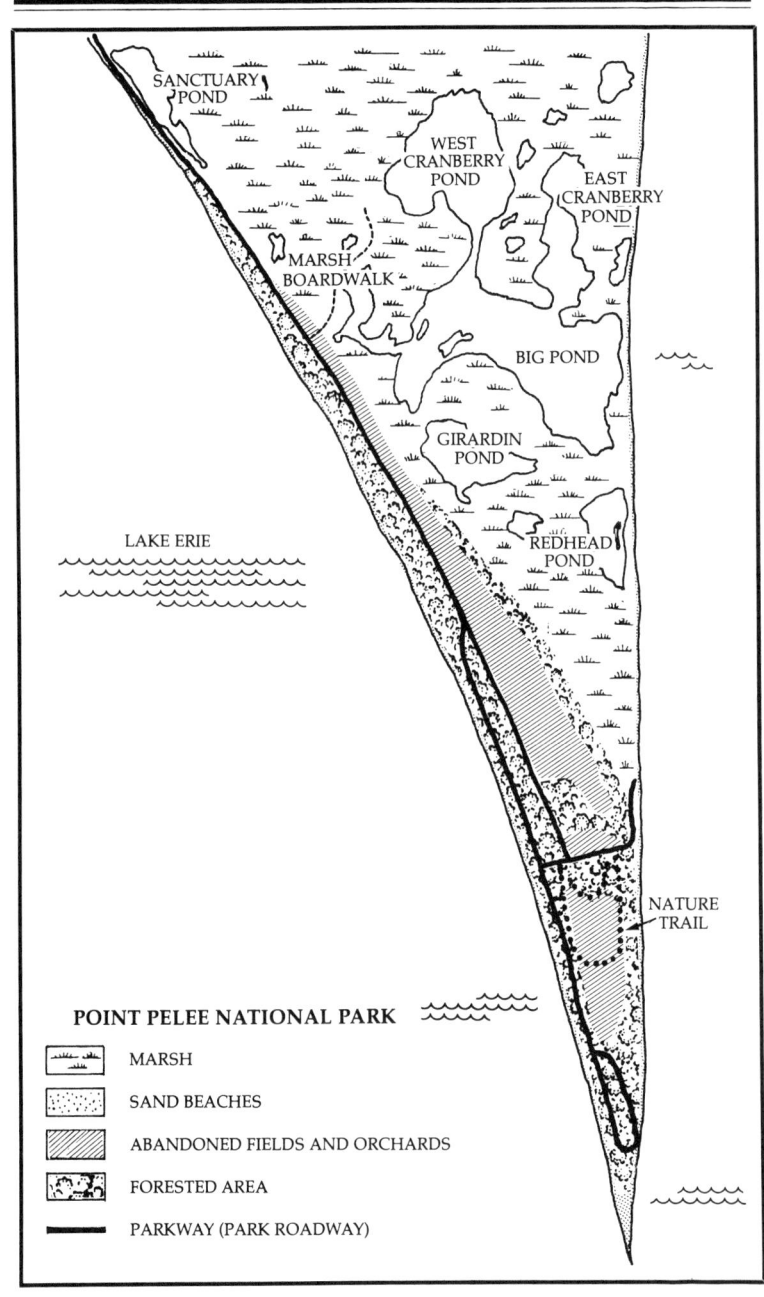

Introduction

Canada is generally considered to be a northern country, and for the most part this is correct. Vast spruce-fir forests extend from coast to coast in a never-ending chain. In the extreme north lie the tundra and high Arctic, a wilderness of ice and snow, almost inaccessible and rarely visited.

There is, however, a small area of Canada with an environment similar to parts of the southern United States, with the same latitude as northern California and the same favourable, balmy weather.

This is Point Pelee, a sandy peninsula in Lake Erie near Leamington, Ontario, that lies farther south than any other part of the Canadian mainland. Remarkably, the 42nd parallel, which forms the northern border of California, also crosses Point Pelee near the park boundary so that nearly all of Point Pelee National Park lies in the same latitude as northern California.

As a result of this location and the modifying influence of the lake that surrounds it, Point Pelee is able to support vegetation and wildlife that are more characteristic of parts of the southern United States than of the rest of Canada.

There is another reason why Point Pelee is of exceptional interest to naturalists: its situation as part of a chain of islands and peninsulas that lie like stepping stones across Lake Erie makes it, every spring and fall, the focus of bird migrations as intense and spectacular as any in North America.

Point Pelee is also one of the few areas where a remnant of southern Ontario's original hardwood forest still survives. When the first settlers arrived in Canada, they found a thickly wooded area of hardwood trees ranging in a continuous belt along the north shore of Lake Erie in southwestern Ontario, extending north to Sarnia and Toronto. This was the only region of eastern deciduous or Carolinian zone forest in Canada. Unfortunately, this unique area was chosen as the centre of urban and industrial development and most of the virgin forest soon came under the axe. Today there are only a few scattered areas where any sizeable hardwood forests still remain in Canada. Point Pelee is one of these.

For an area of such ecological importance, Point Pelee is small. The Point itself is a spit of Eastport sand some nine miles long, jutting into Lake Erie. Not more than a third of the area of the Point, however, is included in the national park, which was established in 1918 specifically to protect and preserve the unique plants and animals of the region. A traverse clay dyke that crosses from shore to shore six miles inland from the tip of the Point forms the northern boundary of the park. The isosceles triangle thus cut off by the dyke has an area of only 6.04 square miles, most of it taken up by a marsh of 2,700 acres. Here the vegetation wages a constant battle with the open ponds which encroach every year on the plants and turn them into thick, green carpets of waterplants. This large marsh with its aquatic plants and animals is a complex and fascinating natural environment. A boardwalk has been built over part of it for the use of visitors.

Over the centuries, the life, death and decay of countless millions of animals and plants will change the marsh to a land environment. As organic debris gathers at the bottom of the ponds, the water becomes shallower. The process, called succession, is exceedingly slow, yet inexorable.

The plant life in the park reflects the influence of a mild, southern climate. Such trees as black walnut, sycamore, white sassafras, shagbark hickory, butternut, hackberry and red cedar are common. Evergreen trees (conifers), so familiar to most Canadians, are almost entirely absent.

The surrounding waters of Lake Erie temper climatic fluctuations and help to give the park one of the longest frost-free growing seasons in Canada. Growth is rapid and lush until late June and provides an abundant and spectacular succession of flowers.

Then, in early summer, hot dry spells usually produce a semi-arid, desert condition. Many herbaceous plants quickly change to a dormant state while some of the shallow-rooted shrubs set winter buds very early and shed much of their foliage. Shrubs often bloom profusely but frequently do not receive enough summer moisture to mature a crop of fruit. Prickly-pear cactus thrives under these circumstances. Its flowers, in late June and early July, attract many visitors to the park. Climbing vines of many kinds festoon the shrubs and trees, making veritable tangles. Athough not usually thought of as part of the woodland scene so far north, lianas drape and hang from many of the tall trees. Grape ivy, poison ivy and Virginia creeper grow in abundance. Among the more notable wildflowers and shrubs are flowering spurge, wild potato vine, swamp mallow, hop tree, spicebush and common cat brier.

Undoubtedly, Point Pelee's greatest claim to fame is as one of the finest birdwatching spots on the continent during the annual migrations, certainly the finest in Canada.

Point Pelee has been of immense interest to naturalists since 1877 when H. Ballou first reported on the impressive autumnal hawk migration. William Brodie, the forerunner of the modern era in Point Pelee's natural history, first visited the area in 1879. William Saunders of London, Ontario, made various trips during and after 1882, and described several bird species that modern naturalists have failed to discover, perhaps because these species no longer inhabit the Point. Later a nucleus of pioneer naturalists who styled themselves the Great Lakes Ornithological Club met as often as feasible between 1905 and 1927 at their headquarters on the East Beach Road of Point Pelee. These six meritorious naturalists, W.E. Saunders, P.A. Taverner, B.H. Swales, J.H. Fleming, A.B. Klugh and J.S. Wallace, have special significance in the annals of Point Pelee.

Point Pelee lies in an area of overlap of the Atlantic and Mississippi flyways – established continental routes along which many birds pass on migration. Tired from the flight across Lake Erie in the spring, many of them stop to rest at the park. An unusual sight for bird watchers occurs when birds can be seen flying south from the point, not in the fall, but in the spring. This 'reverse migration' often occurs when cold weather sets in and the insect population drops, forcing insect-eating birds back south.

From March 15 until June 1, warm air currents carry many rare birds north across Lake Erie to the park where they arrive exhausted and hungry. Birds of all species may be found in profusion. Rarities turn up so often that they are almost taken for granted. The height of the spring migration occurs around mid-May when the warbler wave is under way. At this time the park is literally alive with birds, and the early morning spring choruses have to be heard to be believed. On an especially good day it is possible to record as many as 150 different species of birds, and sometimes in waves of astronomical numbers. As many as 20,000 white-throated sparrows have been observed in a single day, as well as 6,000 red-breasted mergansers, 650 whistling swans, 250 whimbrels, 250 flickers, and 1,000 barn swallows.

The autumn migration southward is also an extremely interesting time at the park. During the latter part of September, large gatherings of hawks, in particular the sharp-shinned

INTRODUCTION

hawk, put on a spectacular show prior to their long flight south. Blue jays, red-winged blackbirds and terns by the hundreds of thousands join with the hawks on their journey southward.

Not all the birds migrate through Point Pelee, for of the 324 species on the park check list, about 90 species stay to nest. Southern birds such as the orchard oriole, Carolina wren, bluegrey gnatcatcher and yellow-breasted chat are summer residents, and in Canada rarely, if ever, breed outside the area of the park. Point Pelee was the first Canadian home of the cardinal, commonly found in the eastern United States. The first native nest was found in the park in 1901; prior to that time it was almost unheard of in Canada, except as a very rare visitor.

A number of mammals also make their home on the Point. Since animals, like plants, depend on a suitable environment for their survival, different animals are found in the different natural environments in the park. Mink and muskrat inhabit the marsh, while the woodland supports deer, coyotes, raccoons, skunks, grey squirrels and cottontail rabbits.

In addition to the typical mammals found at Point Pelee, several rare southern species occur, including the eastern mole, the eastern fox squirrel (on Pelee Island), Baird's deer mouse and the evening bat (only one on record).

Reptiles and amphibians are also very prominent at Point Pelee. In fact, there are probably more turtle species found in the park than anywhere else in Canada, including at least three species entered on the Canadian list of endangered species – the spotted, eastern spiny softshell and Blanding's turtles. The fox snake, another endangered species, is also found here. This is a large snake that may grow to a length of six feet. Other reptile species include the five-lined skink, eastern Canada's only lizard, confined locally to southern Ontario. Fowler's toad, a smaller cousin of the more familiar American toad is native to the park but has not been recorded in recent years.

Largemouth black bass, northern pike and carp are game fish found in the ponds of the large marsh. In spring the run of American smelt, and later, the spawning run of white bass along the shore of Lake Erie, supply good fishing from the beaches in the park. Walleye (locally called pickerel) and yellow perch are caught off-shore. The fishing seasons vary from year to year and park authorities should be consulted for the current regulations. Game fish are not the only fish of interest in the park. Many other species are present including the western lake chubsucker, which was first discovered in Canada in 1949. Butterflies, moths and other insects abound at Point Pelee. The giant swallowtail, our largest native butterfly, is sometimes not uncommon in the park. Point Pelee, and the immediate area, is the only known habitat of this very rare species in Canada.

On the subject of butterflies, one cannot pass over the familiar monarch. In late September huge congregations of migrating monarchs sometimes festoon the shrubs and trees, resting before their long flight to Mexico or southern Florida. When they rise in unison it is a marvellous sight: a mass of orange that delights the eye and gladdens the heart. Other characteristically southern insect inhabitants of Point Pelee include the mole cricket, northern katydid and seaside grasshopper.

During the late spring and summer months, an interpretive service is maintained, and park naturalists are on hand to help with questions and provide organized and illustrated talks and field trips.

Collecting plants and animals is strictly forbidden at Point Pelee, and park wardens are especially alert to any infringement and strongly enforce this ruling. The whole purpose of Point Pelee National Park is to preserve this unique part of Canada's dwindling natural environment and to educate visitors to a better understanding and appreciation of the local natural history.

History of
Point Pelee

Point Pelee has been in existence since the glaciers melted from the area about 10,000 years ago. As the melting icecap receded, its waters picked up sand and dropped it in a ridge extending across the bottom of Lake Erie to the American shore. Through the years wind, waves and lake currents have moved and shaped the sands.

The process is still continuing. Sand is unstable and the land is being built up and at times torn away. Many of the individual plants growing in the park are efficient sand-binders, and in some areas the entire vegetational complex holds the sand in place.

The bedrock of the area is Devonian limestone, laid down in shallow seas 300 million years ago. It is deeply buried under the sand of the park, and no outcrops are seen in the area. Small fossils from this bedrock may be occasionally found on the beaches.

The Point is one link in a chain of stepping stones that lie across Lake Erie. Other links include Pelee, Hen, Middle, and Kelley's Island, the Bass Island, and the south shore peninsula of Marblehead. Together the islands and peninsulas separate the central and west basins of Lake Erie and form a kind of incomplete bridge across the lake. In early history this 'bridge' made crossing the lake feasible for Indian canoeists. The sections of open lake are small, and shelter from unpredictable storms was nearby. Consequently, a well-travelled route developed between Point Pelee and the adjacent mainland, and the south shore of Lake Erie.

Indians were living at Point Pelee about 600 A.D., 400 years before Norse adventurers discovered North America, and approximately 900 years before the epic voyage of Christopher Columbus.

There were at least two major periods of occupation before 1100 A.D., dated at 600 A.D. and 1000 to 1100 A.D. In each of these early occupations the Indians seem to have stayed for only the late spring, summer and autumn months. Archaeologists believe that their shelters were generally temporary, since they found indications of many foundations being built on top of earlier remains. There was little evidence of migratory bird species among the scattered bones around the sites, which suggests that the camps were built after the spring migrations and abandoned before the fall.

The pottery found is an important clue to the origin and culture of these early inhabitants. Pot shards found at Point Pelee represent seven different pottery types, which suggests a fairly complex culture. Pottery found at Point Pelee shows some similarities to shards found at Columbus, Ohio, in Michigan and in northern Ohio. However, the Point Pelee shards are most like finds in upper New York State.

The first white men to see Point Pelee were two Sulpician priests, Fathers Dollier and Galinée, who agreed to accompany Robert Cavalier de la Salle on his planned expedition to the Ohio valley and, he imagined, China.

The expedition left from Montreal on July 5, 1669, with twenty-one men and seven canoes. They travelled via the St. Lawrence River, and in September reached the Iroquois village Tiwanataiva, 12 miles north of present day Hamilton. There they met Joliet, who had been sent by the Governor of New France to explore the Lake Superior region. Joliet told Dollier of a tribe of Indians in the north, the Potawatomi, who had never been visited by a missionary. Dollier then resolved to work among the Potawatomi.

Since this did not coincide with La Salle's purpose, the party split into two groups. Taking seven men and three canoes, Dollier and Galinée left for Lake Erie by way of the Grand River. They followed the northern shore of the lake to the site of the present Port Dover, and wintered there. They set out again on March 23, 1670. Three days later they landed at Point Pelee, having encountered on the way a storm which caused them to lose most of their belongings. Later they made their way through the Detroit River (where they destroyed a stone idol worshipped by the local Iroquois) and continued on their journey to Sault Ste Marie.

La Salle returned safely from his journey to the interior of the continent. Nine years later he constructed, on the shores of the Niagara River above the Falls, a ship of 60 tons, the *Griffon*, the first ship to sail the upper lakes.

On August 7, 1679, La Salle and 34 men sailed from what is now La Salle, New York, bound for Lake Michigan where they planned to trade for furs. They sailed past Point Pelee on August 10, then anchored off the mouth of the Detroit River to pick up fresh supplies. La Salle was most impressed with the abundance of deer and wild turkey.

The *Griffon* proceeded up Lake St Clair to Lake Huron and eventually to Green Bay on Lake Michigan. La Salle loaded the

Griffon with furs and sent it back. The crew was to sell the furs and return the following spring for another load, while La Salle himself remained behind to explore. Mysteriously, however, the *Griffon* disappeared – possibly lost in a storm, or scuttled by a treacherous crew who wished to take the wealth for themselves. Whatever the reason, the *Griffon* was never heard from again.

La Salle set out the following spring for Montreal, travelling across the country to Point Pelee, then by canoe to Niagara. Although he had lost his entire fortune, La Salle had shown that travel by sailing ship on the Great Lakes was possible and had opened the way for later sailors. In the years following La Salle's misadventure, the French used the Great Lakes route by way of Lake Erie more often.

The Point got its name from the early French who landed there. They named it 'pelée' which means 'bare' or 'bald', because the Point was devoid of vegetation, at least on the eastern side.

In 1721 Pierre Francis Xavier Charlevoix, a Jesuit, visited the French colonies in America and returned to France the following year. In his journal, *Journal D'un Voyage dans l'Amerique Septitionale*, he describes Point Pelee:

> 'On the fourth (of June) we spent a good part of the day on a point which runs north and south three leagues and which is called Pointe Pelée. It is however well enough wooded on the west side but the east side is a sandy tract of land with nothing but red cedars that are quite small and not in abundant quantity...There are a great number of bears in this part of the country and last winter more than four hundred were killed on Pointe Pelée alone.'

In 1749 Joseph Gaspard Chassagus de Levy, a military engineer, was sent by the governor of New France, de la Galissoniere, to Detroit. In his account of his journey, de Levy gives extensive detail of his portage across Point Pelee. The portage route, used by the Indians even before the explorers, cut across the middle of the Point from the marsh to the western shore roughly where the entrance to the north-west beach is today. In this way canoeists saved about 10 miles of paddling and avoided the currents at the tip of the point. If de Levy is correct, Point Pelee must have been about one mile longer in 1740 than it is today. He reported that the marsh portage would

Point Pelee from the air

save one and three-fourths leagues of lake travel. This is about 12 miles, two miles more than we would measure for the same route today. De Levy's measurement seems quite reasonable, as Percy Taverner made a similar observation at the turn of the century. De Levy also reported the sandspits at the portage routes to be much wider than at present.

In 1763 during the Pontiac War, Lieutenant Abraham Cuyler's detachment of Royal Americans and Queen's Rangers was attacked on the beach at Point Pelee by Wyandot Indians. Fifty-four men were killed and four were wounded.

In the War of 1812 General Isaac Brock camped at the Point en route to the Fort Detroit and his triumph there over the American general, Hull. In the same war, according to a British loyalist named Parisien, British supply ships bound for Amherstburg had a difficult passage round the Point, where they came under fire from American ships and at the same time risked shipwreck on hidden shoals. Parisien himself met Indians who were bear hunting, and they helped him avoid the Americans by taking him on the portage across the Point Pelee marsh.

Joseph Pickering, an English farmer who travelled through southern Ontario in 1827, recorded this description of Point Pelee:

> ...a great fishing place of the Indians, particularly for sturgeons.

Cedars grow along the sand banks which surround the Point and enclose large ponds and marshes as at Rondeau, and perhaps a greater place for waterfowl.'

A Provincial Surveyer stated in 1851:

'The sand on the Point is composed of sand and gravel. The timber growing on the Point is principally Red Cedar, Juniper, Ash, Hickory, Oak, Sugar Maple, Ironwood and Bass. The sand on the extreme southerly point is movable. There is now a schooner *Emeline* a wreck fixed in the sand.'

Among the first white settlers at Point Pelee were the DeLauriers, who arrived in 1832. The DeLaurier house, built mainly from trees cut in the immediate area, still stands in the park today. Many log houses were built from one particular species of trees, often white pine, maple or elm. The DeLaurier house, however, contains many tree species including white pine, black walnut, and red cedars. In effect, the house is a record of the mixed forest that grew on the Point in the early 1800s. During its history the house has served both as a private residence and as an inn. (At one time early in automobile history a gas pump stood near the road.) The DeLaurier family was very much involved in farming.

The Girardins and other families arrived to settle somewhat later than the DeLauriers. Farming and fishing were the major occupations at Point Pelee. The settlers cleared and drained much of the land on the Point, and evidence of many of their fields can still be seen today.

Major Life Zones

There are approximately seven hundred species of plants at Point Pelee, a substantial number considering that the park covers an area of only six square miles. Several diverse environments and a climate moderated by the lake make it possible for a great number of plants to thrive here. Forest, beach and marsh, and the transition between these three, present a variety of living conditions.

Forest
Forests form the most abundant terrestrial vegetation in the park. Dry upland forests, forming up to 80 percent of the total, occupy higher ground on the western side of the spit and are interspersed with dune grassland, prairies and thickets.

The Point Pelee forest is not mature. It will take centuries of development before it approaches the stability that ecologists call 'climax'. The forest is in the middle stages of development, with many tree species. The maturation process is always slow, but it is particularly slow at Point Pelee. Species of trees which indicate a fully mature forest in this region of the continent are slow to find their way onto this relatively isolated peninsula. Maple and beech, for example, require a well developed soil for growth, and protected, shady ground for seeds to germinate.

To some extent, these conditions are found in the park. Beech trees, however, are not present, and sugar maple trees are found only in small numbers. But in recent years, great numbers of sugar maple seedlings have become established on the west sandspit, and in the north end of the park. Since conditions are apparently suitable now, sugar maple will become a part of the forest canopy in the future.

Change in the forest, within limits, is predictable. Hackberry is quite successful; there are great numbers of mature trees and healthy seedlings that will obviously comprise a significant portion of the park forest for some time. There are also many seedlings of some other trees including sassafras, silver maple, white ash, red oak and shagbark hickory, but these are not as numerous as the hackberry. These trees will not likely be found in great abundance in the future; they are commonly found in more open-grown situations. Some trees, such as tulip, black walnut and chestnut oak seem to be producing few seedlings. It seems that conditions are not entirely suitable for their continued survival here.

The process of change is extremely long and involved. Point

MAJOR LIFE ZONES

Middle stage field

Pelee will retain for many centuries its identity as a host for southern elements. The varied physical environments of the park provide a refuge for many types of plant life. For example, the wetland forest is very different in character from the dry forest. Hackberry, a dry forest tree, can survive only on the ridge tops of wet forest, since it cannot stand the prolonged immersion of its roots in water. Silver maple trees, however, thrive on the wet soil, and can grow on the flooded slacks between the ridges. In some years even the ridge tops may be flooded and some of the hackberry may drown. The character of the wetland forest may be unsettled for many centuries into the future.

The major environments are far from being 'the same' throughout, but on examination, definite patterns in the plant communities can be seen. From place to place there are basic similarities in the types of plants found together. Botanists sometimes term these similar areas 'associations'. In an association, certain species of plants are expected to be found in relation to a certain set of living conditions. Associations are usually named for the most obvious plant(s) present. The term 'association', however, is merely a convenient label, and one association may blend smoothly into the next.

Here are two examples of common plant associations in the park as seen from the Woodland Nature Trail:

1 HACKBERRY FOREST – DRY FOREST:
hackberry (*Celtis occidentalis*), white ash (*Fraxinus americana*), red oak (*Quercus borealis*), basswood (*Tilia americana*), black walnut (*Juglans nigra*), may apple (*Podophyllum peltatum*), sweet cicely (*Osmorhiza longistylis*), herb robert (*Geranium robertianum*), tall bellflower (*Campanula americana*), woodland violet (*Viola spp.*), gooseberry (*Ribes cynosbati*), Virginia creeper (*Parthenocissus quinquefolia*), bur cucumber (*Sicyos angulatus*), and greenbrier (*Smilax hispida*).

2 SILVER MAPLE FOREST – WETLAND FOREST:
silver maple (*Acer saccharinum*), hackberry (*Celtis occidentalis*), sycamore (*Platanus occidentalis*), American elm (*Ulmus americana*), spicebush (*Lindera benzoin*), poison ivy (*Rhus radicans*), Virginia creeper (*Parthenocissus quinquefolia*), jewelweed (*Impatiens biflora*), water plantain (*Alisma [Plantago] aquatica*), duckweed (*Lemna minor*), spring beauty (*Claytonia virginica*), wood nettle (*Laportea canadensis*) and water hemlock (*Cicuta maculata*).

Beach

Since the park is almost six miles long, there are approximately twelve miles of beach. Perhaps more than any other environment of the park, beaches show the one feature of Point Pelee that is constant — change! The shape, width, and steepness of the beaches may be altered completely in a few hours, given a change in the mood of Lake Erie.

The beach environment might be described as a series of bands running roughly parallel to the water's edge. Waves, lapping on the beach, build ridges of pebbles. Often many pebble ridges can be seen, showing how far waves in different winds have reached. The pebbles help collect drifting sand, and provide refuge for insects, insect larvae and spiders.

Life on the open beach is uncertain. During storms waves may crash over the beach face and batter the plant and insect communities. While in summer, the sand may reach 46°C (115°F) in the hot sun, in winter wind-whipped spray may cover the beach in icy armour. Nonetheless, the beach face is far from devoid of life. Even on the most storm-ravaged, people-trodden sections of beach, ants, tiger beetles and spiders can be found. Shorebirds, gulls, terns and crows will not pass up the food tossed by waves upon the shore.

A 'tension zone' exists where the farthest-reaching waves work against the leading edge of the vegetation. Witch grass (*Panicum virgatum*), beard grass (*Andropogon scoparius var. littoralis*), lime grass (*Elymus canadensis*) and hop tree (*Ptelea trifoliata*) thrive on the heated, nutrient-poor soil. Their tough stems and extensive root systems help resist the eroding waves and hold the sand which blows up the beach face. This zone is an arena of struggle, and an important buffer for more delicate plant-animal communities beyond.

Behind the open beach face lies a complex community closely resembling that of dry old fields. Red cedar (*Juniperus virginiana*), staghorn sumac (*Rhus typhina*), Canada blue grass (*Poa compressa*) and wormwood (*Artemisia caudata*) are common. The soil is progressively richer and more moist inland, so that the area blends subtly into the forest. Animal life abounds, since the protection of the forest, and the food of the area itself, are immensely attractive.

Here are two major, common plant associations of the Point Pelee beach area:

1 HOP TREE – DUNE GRASS,
LEADING EDGE OF VEGETATION ALONG BEACHES:
hop tree (*Ptelea trifoliata*), panic grass (*Panicum virgatum*), beard grass (*Andropogon scoparius var. littoralis*), Canada lime grass (*Elymus canadensis*) and frost grape (*Vitis vulpina*).

2 RED CEDAR – SUMAC,
BETWEEN LEADING EDGE OF VEGETATION AND FOREST (WEST SHORE) OR MARSH (EAST):
red cedar (*Juniperus virginiana*), staghorn sumac (*Rhus typhina*), fragrant sumac (*R. aromatica*), hackberry (*Celtis occidentalis*), black willow (*Salix nigra*), panic grass (*Panicum virgatum*), Canada blue grass (*Poa compressa*), frost grape (*Vitis vulpina*), beard grass (*Andropogon scoparius var. littoralis*), poison ivy (*Rhus radicans*), wormwood (*Artemesia caudata*) and hoary puccoon (*Lithospermum canescens*).

Marsh

The marsh is by far the largest life zone in the park, and covers four of its six square miles. Early in Point Pelee's history the east and west sandspits grew lakeward from the mainland. The water level in the marsh varies from day to day and season to season. These variations are caused by rainfall, and by fluctuating water levels in Lake Erie. Although most forms of life seem to adjust well to changing water levels, the living community may be affected. For example, in low water years, mud flats are exposed, and more nesting platforms for coots, terns and rails may be provided. Populations of food plants change with water levels; some plants need shallow water; and others deeper water.

Patience and stealth on the marsh boardwalk bring results, especially early in the day, when animal life is active. Turtles, frogs and snakes hunt in the shallows, or along the edge of the cattail mat. Raccoons, weasels, and mink are part of the complex energy and food web, which includes all marsh life. On quiet evenings one can hear muskrats munching cattails or spadderdock roots. Bowfin, carp, northern pike, grass pike and largemouth bass are some of the larger fish that are frequently seen cruising the ponds. Painted, spotted, musk, Blanding's and snapping turtles lurk in their favourite haunts. With such a variety of living things, the marsh is an experience that can never be stale.

Here are two common marsh plant associations that can be seen from the boardwalk:

1 CATTAIL MAT:
broadleaf cattail (*Typha latifolia*), narrowleaf cattail (*Typha angustifolia*), skull-cap mink (*Scutellaria galericulata*), marsh milkweed (*Asclepias incarnata*), swamp loose-strife (*Decodon verticillatus*), swamp rose-mallow (*Hibiscus palustris*) and jewel-weed (*Impatiens biflora*).

2 SPADDERDOCK – PONDWEED:
spadderdock (*Nuphar advena*), pondweed (*Potamogeton spp.*) water lily (*Nyphaea odorata*), water shield (*Brazenia schreberi*), bladderwort (*Utricularia vulgaris*), pickerel weed (*Pontederia cordata*), water-weed (*Anacharis canadensis*) and bulrush (*Scirpus americanus*).

Field & Orchard

Farming was once a major occupation at Point Pelee, and much of the land was cleared and drained for that purpose. Orchards occupied large areas of land, and evidence of many farm fields can still be seen.

Now that farming has ceased, the fields and orchards are gradually returning to their natural state. The process whereby land, once forest, is cleared and then allowed to become forest again is called 'secondary succession'.

The type of plants that grow on the soil appear in a very orderly sequence. Those that require bare soil and full sunlight are found first. By their very presence they add to the soil with a litter of leaves, stems and roots. Their shade provides refuge for plants that cannot tolerate the open harsh conditions. Gradually the soil develops, the shade is more complete, and entirely different plants are found. A forest develops from the field. Its character is like that of the forest nearby, since the older forest is a source of seed supply. The patterns in development tell us much of the processes of natural regeneration.

Today, very little of Essex County remains forested. Most of the land was cleared by 1900. Point Pelee remains as an example of the once abundant forest of the area.

Introduced Plants

The introduction of exotic, extirpated and unusual species has occurred at Point Pelee since it first became a national park. Extensive plantings, especially of hackberry, occurred in the 1920s, but their extent and the degree to which they have affected natural plant communities have not been ascertained.

Large scale plantings of black walnut have also been made in several locations in the park and the influence on the forest communities will not become apparent for several years. The Oregon grape (*Mahonia aquifolia*) and several horticultural varieties of *Juniperus* have been planted beside buildings and parking lots.

Major plantings have been made of more than 10,000 white pine (*Pinus strobus*) and red oak (*Quercus rubra*) as well as white poplar (*Populus alba*), white willow (*Salix alba*) and cherry (*Prunus cerasus*). Also, more than 2,000 white oak (*Quercus alba*) have been introduced. Other introductions that can be considered here are the adventives or weeds, inadvertently brought into the park by both natural agencies and man. These include timothy grass (*Phleum pratense*), Italian millet (*Setaria italica*), shepherd's purse (*Capsella bursa-pastoris*) and many others. Some say that milkweed (*Asclepias syriaca*) was planted on the Point for latex production during the war years but there are no written reports of the operation.

Even with weeds some southern species are casuals at Point Pelee. As the preservation of natural ecosystems is a generally accepted purpose of national parks the implications of future large-scale plantings of trees and other plants at Point Pelee should be considered.

Rare and Extinct Plant Species

Many of the plant species recorded as rare or endangered in Point Pelee National Park are important components of marsh and forest habitats, and their decline has meant impoverishment of these communities. Burning bush (*Euonymus atropurpureus*) and rattlesnake fern (*Botrychium virginianum*) within the woodlands, and the moss (*Climacium dendroides*) and alternate leaved dogwood (*Cornus alternifolia*) in the marshlands are regarded as endangered in the park, but are common in suitable habitats outside.

There are large numbers of aquatic species that appear to be declining that were previously recorded as common. Among these are the common reed (*Phragmites communis*), two species of bur-reed (*Sparganium eurycarpum* and *S. americaum*) and both species or subspecies of wild rice (*Zizania sp.*). The sweet flag (*Acorus calamus*) is decreasing at several stations along the Lake Erie shoreline and it is rare now at Point Pelee.

There are some twenty or thirty species that are rare in

Flowers at Point Pelee

Canada but found at Point Pelee. The status of *Cerastrium arvense var. oblongifolium* is of particular concern; only one clump is known at Point Pelee. The decline of populations of some species has been accelerated by human interference. This is particularly the case with two species – blue or four-angled ash and the prickly-pear cactus (*Opuntia humifusa*).

Prickly-pear cactus thrives in the semi-arid conditions found in the park. Its large yellow flowers, which open in late June or early July, attract many visitors and photographers to the Woodland Trail. This is the only place in eastern Canada where extensive patches of this southern novelty persist.

Other Canadian rarities which may be endangered include the marsh or swamp mallow (*Hibiscus palustris*) and the wild potato vine (*Opomaea pandurata*), both of which are found at Point Pelee as components of natural ecosystems.

The lack of good early information on the presence and abundance of plants within the park area makes it difficult to examine records of extirpated species. Usually information is limited to more obvious species of trees. The pawpaw (*Asimia triloba*) was previously recorded as abundant but is very rare or extinct today. Redbud was apparently extirpated and then reintroduced.

The tuliptree (*Liriodendron tulipfera*) was formerly represented by only one tree on a farm but it is now somewhat more common.

Some researchers have suggested that some other endangered species may now have become extinct. These include sessile-fruiting arrowhead (*Sagittaria heterophylla*), bur-reed (*Sparganium americanum*) and Indian rice (*Zizania plaustris*). Some of the aquatic species which were thought possibly extirpated in recent years may be reintroduced by natural means, such as waterfowl.

The extinction of a species, even if it appears insignificant, is a serious and irreparable loss. It means ecological readjustment and a lessening of natural diversity. Extinction of plant species from Canada is difficult to ascertain because of the lack of reliable information. Southern Ontario has probably seen the extinction of several southern species of plants in post-glacial times. None of the plants that have been found at Point Pelee is now recorded as totally extinct, although several extinctions from Canada are known. Some of these have been reintroduced. The round-leaved green briar (*Simlax rotundifolia*) was formerly recorded from Point Pelee and one other location in Essex County but has not been seen for some years and may be extinct. The orchid (*Habenaria ciliaris*), once reported just north of the park, has not been found recently in Canada.

Birds

Cedar Waxwing

BIRDS

Point Pelee National Park, in a sense, owes its existence to migrant and resident bird life. Noted ornithologists such as Percy Taverner, William Brodie and William Saunders early recognized Point Pelee as important and unique in the migration patterns of Canada. Saunders introduced the Great Lakes Ornithological Club to Point Pelee. In subsequent field trips its members noticed the typical 'wave' migration with·great numbers of individual species and a great variety of bird life.

Birdwatchers today follow the footsteps of these noted ornithologists who first visited the Point in the late 1870s. The park now probably attracts more birdwatchers and ornithologists than any other small area in Canada. At the time of writing, about 336 species of birds have been noted at Point Pelee since records have been kept, beginning in 1879. Many of these birds are rarely seen in other parts of Canada.

The list of extremely rare migrants that have been observed in the park is most impressive and includes: blue grosbeak (*Guiraca caerulea*), Bell's vireo (*Vireo bellii*), snowy egret (*Leucophoyx thula*), Kirtland's warbler (*Dendroica kirtlandii*), yellow-throated warbler (*Dendroica dominica*), worm-eating warbler (*Helmitheros vermivorus*), Cassin's sparrow (*Aimophila cassinii*), glossy ibis (*Plegadis falcinellus*), ruff (*Philomachus pugnax*), Bachman's sparrow (*Aimophila aestivalis*), Townsend's solitaire (*Myadestes townsendi*), American avocet (*Recurvirostra americana*), mountain bluebird (*Sialia currucoides*), yellow-headed blackbird (*Xanthocephalus xanthocephalus*), white pelican (*Pelecanus erythrorhynchos*), western kingbird (*Tyrannus verticalis*), marbled godwit (*Limosa fedoa*), Hudsonian godwit (*L. haemastica*), western sandpiper (*Ereunetes mauri*) and Sabine's gull (*Xema sabini*). Point Pelee also has the distinction of being the only Canadian locality that can claim to have harboured Virginia's warbler (*Vermivora virginiae*), and Bewick's wren (*Thryomanes bewickii*). Chuck-Will's widow (*Caprimulgus Carolinensis*) has been found, in Canada, only on Point Pelee and on Pelee Island.

Migration patterns have remained much the same over the years, with arrival and departure dates varying by only a few days. Point Pelee is a focal point in migration. Southward migrating birds are funnelled to the Pelee peninsula: the tip of the lake-bordered Ontario peninsula. This area lies along both the Mississippi and Atlantic flyways, and is frequented by species nesting from the prairies to Quebec and the Arctic. Detailed records kept over the years emphasize Point Pelee's position on the two flyways. Birds normally found far to the east or west of the region occasionally migrate through the park.

For most birds, Point Pelee is not a destination, but a stopover during migration. Only about 90 species of the 324 species sighted are known to have nested in the park. One important reason for the popularity of Point Pelee with both migrating and nesting birds is habitat diversity: the strikingly different environments on the Point are suitable for many different species of birds.

Reverse migration, a phenomenon demonstrated by many species, has been studied for some time at Point Pelee, where it occurs regularly. In reverse migration, birds are observed flying in the direction opposite to that which is expected for the time of year. Red-winged blackbirds, barn swallows, starlings, American goldfinches, grackles and chimney swifts are the most common of the many birds observed in reverse migration.

Migrating birds do not all arrive in a steady flow, as each species has a migration pattern of its own. Why a wave of birds descends on Point Pelee during any particular night is not fully understood. The phenomenon is not peculiar to this area but occurs in the general pattern of migration in eastern North America.

A wave of migration seems to occur when a warm weather front advancing from the southeast meets a cold weather front coming from the northeast. If the two fronts meet at ground level, or the warm front overrides the cold front, the birds will descend. In the latter case the rising warm air becomes cooler with the increasing altitude until it is finally too cold for the birds and they descend. The warm front in its northward journey has to pass over an area where migrating birds are present in order to carry them with it.

During the spring migration, the influx of birds is first noted in March with the arrival of the whistling swan and other waterfowl. Horned larks, flickers, red-winged blackbirds, eastern bluebirds and fox sparrows also reach their maximum numbers in March. April is the month of arrival and of peak numbers for the horned grebes, double-crested cormorants, American coots, common terns, eastern phoebes and many of the sparrows. In May the white-crowned and white-throated sparrows arrive. The latter part of the month is shore bird time when both plovers and sandpipers are at their maximum numbers. The black-and-white warblers and the yellow-rumped warblers appear

Promonotary Warbler

early in the month and warbler migration is nearly over when the blackpoll appears. All migration is over in early June.

There is usually a special day when particular bird species are conspicuous and present in large numbers. These are popularly referred to as 'big days'. There have been big days for the following: 20,000 white-throated sparrows, 6,000 red-breasted mergansers, 1,000 barn swallows, 650 whistling swans, 250 whimbrels, 250 flickers and 10 Carolina wrens. These are but a few examples.

Spotting rare birds is an especially exciting event for birdwatchers. Since 1906 confirmed sightings of 26 species rare to southern Ontario have been recorded in the park, mainly during spring migration. Some of these such as Virginia's warbler, yellow-throated warbler, scissor-tailed flycatcher, Bachman's sparrow, glossy ibis, Sabine's gull and Cassin's sparrow have strayed for one reason or another far out of their range. But others such as the worm-eating warbler, white-eyed vireo (*Vireo griseus*), blue grosbeak and summer tanager (*Piranga rubra*), seen in the context of passing years, may be in the process of extending their range into southern Ontario.

The first Canadian nesting records for the cardinal and the Carolina wren were at Point Pelee in 1901 and 1906, respectively. These species have since managed to spread into more northern areas. Clearing of the forest, amelioration of southern Ontario's climate during the present century, and surplus population of the birds themselves have all been suggested as possible reasons for the northward shift in the ranges of many species.

One cannot imagine a more desirable addition to our fauna than the cardinal (*Cardinalis cardinalis*), with its brilliant red plumage, black face and jaunty crest. It is now prevalent south of Georgian Bay and west of Hastings County, but it was a rare bird in the province prior to the turn of the century. The first active cardinal's nest was discovered at Point Pelee in 1901. The cardinal had reached Chatham as a nesting bird by 1909, London by 1915, Brantford by 1919 and Toronto by 1922.

William Brodie became aware of the cardinal at Point Pelee as early as July, 1879, during his first visit to the park:

> 'I formed a speaking acquaintance with several people and all had a story to tell about a visitation of 'war-birds' a few weeks previously. From descriptions given there was no doubt these 'war-birds' were cardinals.'

However, William Saunders in his subsequent visits to Point Pelee between 1882 and 1900 had found no evidence of cardinals. According to Percy Taverner, this lack of evidence points to the conclusion that the cardinal occupied Point Pelee until at least 1879, and then apparently deserted the locality until the turn of the century. During the spring of 1907 both he and Saunders were at the Point and this time cardinals were heard whistling all around them.

Cardinals received a big boost in the autumn of 1938, when there was a mass influx in the Niagara area. This mass influx of cardinals resulted in the first breeding records for many areas in the southern counties of Ontario. Just how far cardinals will expand into Ontario beyond their present limits nobody knows, but this extension of their range is expected to continue. The cardinal has also nested in Winnipeg and has summered in Montreal.

Like the cardinal, the Carolina wren's (*Thryothorus ludovicianus*) first Canadian nesting was also at Point Pelee. On

Cardinal

Mockingbird

September 6, 1905, N.B. Klugh collected a young Carolina wren from a thicket on the east shore, about two miles from the end of the Point. Subsequent nestings were to follow. This species' occupation of our southern counties has been at a much slower rate than the cardinal's, but it has nested as far east as Canton in Durham County.

According to Taverner, Carolina wrens were quite common at Point Pelee and Pelee Island, but after 1913 they seemed to become more rare. The species is now well established again at the Point, frequenting the densest woodland where it is more often heard than seen. The song of the Carolina wren is perfectly distinct and quite unlike any other heard in the park area.

The mockingbird (*Mimus polyglottos*) is another transplanted American. Again, the first Ontario breeding on record occurred at Point Pelee in 1909. There was, however, a previously known occurrence of this species in the park, on May 20, 1906, when a male bird was taken near an old orchard on the west side about five miles from the Point. A search was made for a possible mate, but to no avail.

The mockingbird is still rare in Ontario but it has nested as far north as Manitoulin Island and as far east as Kingston. The fact that it has nested near Montreal suggests that it may breed anywhere between the Detroit and Ottawa Rivers.

Bewick's wren (*Thryomanes bewickii*) is another southern wren species that has made its home at Point Pelee in recent years. On May 20, 1950, Dr W.H.H. Gunn found four Bewick's wren eggs in a nest on a beam under a cottage in the park. Three of these eggs were sent to the Royal Ontario Museum. This was the first Ontario nesting record for Bewick's wren in its only known Canadian locality. Three more nests were subsequently discovered under the eaves of an open pavilion near the tip of the Point in 1957.

The following species are also rare summer residents of Point Pelee. They have all bred within the park area at one time or another since 1879. Many of these are almost entirely restricted to the park and environs, and are unheard of elsewhere in Canada.

Formerly, piping plovers (*Charadrius melodus*) nested on most of the large, gravelly beaches along Lakes Ontario, Erie and Huron. When Taverner and Swales made their early visits to the park from 1882 to 1887, they regarded this species as a common summer resident and regular breeder on the east beach at Point Pelee.

The last breeding record for the piping plover at Point Pelee was in 1938; it is not known to have bred in the park since that time. Unfortunately, this is one species that has not been able to cope with man and his increasing use of the lake beaches. This bird gets its name from its call, a low-pitched, musical whistle.

The largest of the wood warblers, the yellow-breasted chat (*Icteria virens*), breeds very locally in Canada in extreme southwestern Ontario, southern British Columbia, southeastern Alberta and southern Saskatchewan. Point Pelee is the only place in Canada where this species is any more than an accidental straggler. The first observation of the yellow-breasted chat in Canada was probably made in the park. William Brodie recorded an account of his July trip of 1879 and mentioned that a dead bird of this species, recently killed in an unfortunate accident, was brought to him by some school children.

The chat appears to be a bird of secretive habits. It leaves early in the season and steals away so quietly that it is rarely noticed during the fall migration. There is a breeding record for the yellow-breasted chat at Point Pelee in 1950.

The dickcissel (*Spiza americana*) is a very rare summer resident of extreme southwestern Ontario. It is a bird that, after initially extending its range, retreated again.

William Saunders reported that it was common at Point Pelee in 1884, and that several of these birds were found in a meadow about two miles from the end of the Point. 'These birds were observed in every locality in the park, and on the return trip they were heard constantly.' This was the first Canadian record.

From that time on practically nothing was heard of the bird until 1895, when it suddenly spread over the peninsula. Many of the then small number of ornithologists found it in their vicinity, and a pair of the dickcissels actually spent the summer as far north as Ottawa. But the next year they were gone, and with the exception of five specimens observed by Saunders at Point Pelee on September 10, 1900, and a small colony reported at Rondeau Park about 1935, only a casual pair has been seen.

The blue-grey gnatcatcher (*Polioptila caerulea caerulea*) was formerly far more plentiful in the park area than it is today. Both Saunders and Taverner reported this species as very common at Point Pelee and the environs in the late 1800s. Saunders once found three nests of gnatcatchers in a single morning in a wood near London, Ontario, after finding his first nest there in 1874. Today the blue-gray gnatcatcher is a very rare breeding summer resident in Point Pelee National Park.

In Canada, the orchard oriole (*Icterus spurius*) is found only along the southern edge of Ontario. This species was first mentioned by Saunders at Point Pelee in 1884. Taverner reported that he found the orchard oriole to be abundant during his first visit on May 13, 1905, and on subsequent May trips, it outnumbered the northern (Baltimore) oriole perhaps two to one. The farmers of that time were well acquainted with the orioles, and called this species the 'oriole' while the northern was generally known as the 'golden robin'. L.L. Snyder found an orchard oriole's nest and three eggs plus a cowbird's egg at Point Pelee on June 14, 1920.

The prothonotary warbler (*Protonotaria citrea*) has nested at a few places along the north shore of Lake Erie. Summer reports from Bruce and York Counties indicate that its foothold in

BIRDS

Saw Whet Owl

southern Ontario as a breeding bird, may be more extensive than is known at present.

Its principal habitat has always been Rondeau Provincial Park, in Kent County, where the environment would certainly appear to be more suitable than at Point Pelee. There were an estimated 100 pairs present at Rondeau Park in June, 1933, but only a small fraction of that number exists there today. During the depression days of the mid 1930's a clean-up programme was organized to make work for the unemployed. This operation eliminated suitable nesting sites for the warblers.

Breeding records for the prothonotary warbler in Point Pelee National Park were made in 1955, in 1976 and, possibly, in 1977.

The tufted titmouse (*Parus bicolor*) is a bird species that is more abundant south of the Canadian border. It was first reported in Ontario on May 2, 1914, when William Saunders and J.S. Wallace saw two specimens at Point Pelee. It has since extended its range northward and eastward.

That the tufted titmouse is spreading in southern Ontario is evident from the records. From 1914 to 1960 there were only 92 reports of titmice in the province, then during the winter of 1961 and 1962, a total of 64 were recorded from fifty-two different locations in southern Ontario. There was only one report from Point Pelee, however.

Tufted Titmouse

Bald Eagle

    As with the cardinal, mockingbird and Carolina wren, most Ontario tufted titmouse observations have been in winter. This fact supports the supposition that pioneers in taking over new territory may be young birds.

    The largest and most magnificent of Canadian birds of prey, the bald eagle (*Haliaeetus leucocephalus*), was formerly widespread throughout the continent. It has, unfortunately, become increasingly rare over most of its range. This is largely because the dead and dying fish on which it feeds have accumulated sublethal doses of chlorinated hydrocarbon pesticide poisons. The result has been infertile eagle eggs.

    The bald eagle was formerly an uncommon permanent resident at Point Pelee National Park, and was seen less often during the summer months. A pair of these birds bred annually near the base of the Point, and Percy Taverner reported on May 13, 1905, a nest in a tall tree about a mile inland. During all his visits to Point Pelee, he noted from one to four eagles almost daily. During the autumnal flights of the sharp-shinned hawks, the eagles were so pestered by these aggressive little birds, that the eagles were forced to move away from the vicinity.

    Bald eagles were certainly known to have bred in the park in the 1930s, and were known to have resided there well into the 1950s. There were reports, through the 1950s, of an occupied nest at Point Pelee. Eagles are supposed to have disappeared

Red-tailed Hawk

from Point Pelee when their nest tree was blown over in the early 1960s, according to W. Wyett, former head park naturalist.

The autumn migration of birds at Point Pelee is probably the most impressive of its kind that can be seen in Canada or even in North America, and compares favourably with the northerly spring migration. Nowhere else can one observe at such close range the migrational flights of birds of prey, and the reactions of various small birds as they attempt to elude capture. On a good day, a thousand or more sharp-shinns may be seen flying up and down the Point, or leaving its tip to fly over Lake Erie. The populations may build rapidly from September 7th until the peak of migration, usually around September 16th to September 18th. Even as late as October 17th, up to a hundred a day might be seen.

William Saunders first saw the flight of the sharp-shinned hawks in 1882 and described it in such glowing terms that it seems like an exaggeration:

> 'There were more sharp-shinns than one would suppose were in Ontario, and one day my brother and I stood thirty paces apart, facing each other, with the double-barrel, breech-loaders, and for a short time the hawks passed so thick that we had to let some go by unmolested because we could not load fast enough to fire at each as they came.'

Other hawks use Point Pelee as a migratory route but the sharp-shinned hawk is by far the most numerous. 'Big days' for other hawks have been: goshawk 4, Cooper's hawk 150, red-tailed hawk 50, red-shouldered hawk 50, broad-winged hawk 400, rough-legged hawk 41, golden eagle 2, bald eagle 4, osprey 5, peregrine falcon 6, pigeon hawk (merlin) 6 and American kestrel 17.

The fall migration of the blue jay is also an impressive sight. This species is fairly large, brilliantly coloured and noisy. A concentration of these birds such as occurs at Point Pelee, when from 1,000 to 10,000 a day may be seen, is a spectacular event never to be forgotten. From early morning to dusk you know by sight and sound that blue jays are present in large numbers. They fly up and down the length of the Point and sometimes mill around the terminal area. They go out over the water a certain distance and then return. They may do this a number of times and may or may not leave. When the sharp-shinned

Sharp-shinned Hawk

hawks and the blue jays are both abundant, one can watch the jays elude the hawks, usually with success, and seemingly delighting in this dangerous game.

Large flocks of blackbirds, starlings and crows also migrate through Point Pelee in the fall. They feed on corn-in-the-ear and other grains, and thus cause serious losses to the farmer. Their role as a nuisance is not new, for de Levy reported that in 1749 blackbirds were injurious to the grain crops of the settlers near what is now Windsor. The birds were so plentiful that persons had to be assigned to guard the crops. The following 'big days' for some blackbird species have been recorded: common grackles 20,000, rusty blackbirds 2,000, and brown-headed cowbirds 10,000. The greatest number of red-winged blackbirds seen at the Point was on November 17, 1949, when it was estimated that 250,000 birds were present.

Hummingbirds are also common migrants through the park during late August and early September. Unlike blue jays, they have no qualms about crossing Lake Erie. They course down the shore, and without hesitation, start out across the lake. Unlike most birds, they fly low, just above the shoreline and water, and sometimes even within the troughs of the waves.

Point Pelee is one of the three or four places in Ontario where saw-whet owls may be seen in migration. But you have to look for them at the proper date, the proper time and the proper place. A small migration usually goes through the park between October 5th and October 30th. The best way to find them is to use a flashlight and to search red cedar trees at the south end of the park.

Other kinds of birds such as bobolinks, meadowlarks and cedar waxwings may be seen at Point Pelee in numbers. One is indeed lucky to be in the park when a wave of migrating birds are passing through. Whether it is the wood warblers in the spring or the sharp-shinned hawks in the fall, there is no better birding anywhere. The following is a list of groups of birds, and approximate dates of migration through Point Pelee:

SPRING

	Start of build up	Peak
Loon and grebes	April 1	April 15
Swans, geese and ducks	April 10	April 20
Shorebirds	May 5	May 20
Gulls	March 20	April 10
Terns	April 15	May 1
Cuckoos Hummingbirds Flycatchers Swallows Jays Thrushes Wrens Waxwings Vireos Warblers Finches	May 5	May 15

FALL

	Start of build up	Peak
Ducks	Sept 10	Sept 30
Geese	Oct 10	Oct 20
Hawks	Oct 25	Nov 10
Shorebirds	Sept 10	Sept 20
Yellowlegs Pectoral Sandpiper Sanderling	July 30	Aug 5
Plovers	Oct 1	Oct 10
Terns	Aug 25	Sept 10
Cuckoos Hummingbirds Flycatchers Wrens Vireos Warblers	Aug 15	Sept 5
Owls	Oct 15	Oct 25
Blackbirds Sparrows	Oct 15	Oct 30
Thrushes	Sept 15	Sept 25

Mammals

The various life zones at Point Pelee – forest, beach and marsh support a diverse mammalian population.

Most of the mammals found in the park are resident for the entire year. As far as the mammals are concerned, Point Pelee is as isolated as if it were an island. To the north of the park lies dyked and open farmland and an extensively developed cottage area. The lake, on the other two sides of the triangular park area, is a barrier for all but the bats. Animals very seldom move in or out of the park, although on a few rare occasions deer, coyote, fox, rabbits and weasels have been seen entering or leaving.

Over the years the population of mammals at Point Pelee has been modified by hunting, trapping, marsh draining and land clearing. Some animals, such as the beaver, timber wolf, black bear, marten, fisher, cougar, Canada lynx, bobcat and the now extinct eastern wapiti, have completely disappeared from the area as a result of these pressures. Others, including the cottontail rabbit, the eastern mole and the white-tailed deer, have taken advantage of the newly cleared land to establish themselves.

Each mammal is adapted to a particular environment and has particular requirements for food, shelter, protection and social interaction. If these requirements cannot be filled – if, for example, there are critical changes in the environment – then the mammal will probably not survive in the area.

In the park, there are restrictions on the mammal population, imposed by man's use of the land. Roadways, parking lots and building sites tend to limit the movements of some animals. There are additional environmental limits on animal distribution imposed by other physical barriers. The marsh may prove to be a barrier to movement by some terrestrial mammals. On a smaller scale, open fields prove to be a barrier to woodland mice, while forested areas limit the spread of the meadow vole.

The following mammals either have been found in Point Pelee National Park, or have a current distribution that includes the park and might therefore occur there now or in the future.

Marsupials (Order *Marsupialia*)
Virginia Opossum (*Didelphis marsupialis*)
The common or Virginia opossum is North America's only marsupial. Although not currently found at Point Pelee, it has appeared sporadically in Essex County in Ontario since 1850.

This species' most recent invasion of Ontario from the south has continued since 1947. Now opossums are quite common in certain areas adjacent to Lake Erie. There has even been an extension of their range across the St Lawrence River and into southeastern Ontario.

This attractive animal, well-known for its habits of playing dead and carrying its young in an abdominal pouch, would make a most interesting addition to the park's mammalian fauna.

Shrews and moles (Order *Insectivora*)
Of the four shrew species that might occur within the park – the common, smoky, big short-tailed and little short-tailed shrews – only two, the common and big short-tailed, have been recorded. The little short-tailed shrew (*Cryptosis parva*) is an open grassland species and has been found in Canada only at Long Point in Norfolk County, Ontario. Further study may establish its presence and that of the smoky shrew (*Sorex fumeus*) at Point Pelee.

Common or Masked Shrew (*Sorex cinerus*)
The smallest mammal found at Point Pelee, the common shrew is less than four inches (10 cm) long from nose to tip of tail. This tiny animal uses tremendous amounts of energy, and often consumes more than its own body weight in food each day. The common shrew has very broad habitat requirements, and at Point Pelee it is found in wet forest, dry forest, dunes, fields and older sections of the marsh. It may be found above ground, in the burrows of other animals and in those of its own making. It feeds on insects and other invertebrates, on plant matter and on the flesh of some vertebrates.

Big Short-Tailed Shrew (*Blarina brevicauda*)
The big short-tailed shrew is the largest of Canadian shrews. It is commonly found in the forest where it burrows underground or under leaf-litter. Insects and other invertebrates comprise the mainstay of its diet, although plant matter is also included. This animal has a defense mechanism in the form of glands which emit strong, pungent odours, and submaxillary glands which emit a poison used to immobilize its prey.

Eastern Mole (*Scalopus aquaticus*)
The eastern mole is found in Canada only in the sandy soil of Ontario's Essex County. It is very common at Point Pelee. One can see the moles' runways on lawns, open areas and in open

woods. This is one of the largest of mole species; it grows to an overall length of about eight inches (20 cm). Its diet consists mainly of earthworms and soil insects, but it also eats other invertebrates and some vegetable matter.

Both the forefeet and the hind feet of this mole show indications of webbing between the toes. This characteristic led Linneaus to believe that this species was aquatic, and so he called it *aquaticus*. In fact, the eastern mole is probably the most subterranean of North American moles, and only rarely will it emerge from underground.

The eastern mole is especially well adapted for life underground, with broad, clawed feet, a snout, a muscular body, and fur that brushes forward and backward equally well. The eyes have become degenerate small black balls embedded in the skin beneath minute hairless eyelids, and have moved forward out of the regular sockets to be on the side of the snout.

In the United States the eastern mole is considered a nuisance in parks, gardens, lawns and golf courses, and control measures are often called for. In Canada its range is too restricted to cause concern. At Point Pelee predation by man is the chief threat to this mole's survival.

Eastern Mole

MAMMALS

Bats (Order *Chiroptera*)
Point Pelee falls within the range of eight species of bats: the little brown, eastern long-eared, least, silver-haired, western pipistrelle, big brown, red and hoary. There are records of four of these species having been collected in the park, as well as a single record of the evening bat whose normal range lies somewhat south of the park area. Red bats and silver-haired bats are known to migrate through Point Pelee in spring and fall. Migrating hoary bats possibly pass through the park as well. The others mentioned are hibernators. Bats deserve a much better reputation for they are of immense benefit to man; their food consists entirely of flying insects, which they consume in large quantities.

The little brown, least and big brown bats occasionally roost in buildings. The big brown bats may also hibernate in buildings, thus bringing them into contact with man.

Little Brown Bat (*Myotis lucifugus*)
The little brown bat is the most common bat in eastern Canada. This bat roosts in caves and hibernates in buildings. Hibernating sites must be cool but not below freezing. This species is most active just after dark, and feeds on the wing through woods or over fields and marsh. These bats consume large numbers of mosquitoes, moths, and other insects.

Silver-Haired Bat (*Lasionycteris noctivagans*)
A migratory and solitary bat, the silver-haired bat is not usually found in Canada in the winter. It does not frequent buildings, but is found in trees during the daylight hours. Congregations and flights of these migrating bats have been seen at Point Pelee.

Big Brown Bat (*Eptesicus fuscus fuscus*)
The big brown bat is a hibernator that occupies cool buildings and caves during winter. Like other bats that rely on buildings and caves, it is rarely found in the park because there are few suitable sites. During the summer this bat may use both buildings and trees as roosting sites.

This species constitutes a grave public health menace because it is the most common rabies carrier. The first known case of a rabid bat in eastern Canada was noted in the Toronto area in the autumn of 1961 and was attributed to this species.

Red Bat (*Lasiurus borealis*)
Forests are the preferred habitat of the red bat, especially forests near water. This is the most common bat species at Point Pelee.

The proximity of marsh and forest in the park provides suitable food and hunting conditions, and a suitable roost. On clouded days these bats have occasionally been seen flying in the park. Red bats migrate through Point Pelee in larger numbers than any other species.

It was expected that the red bat might become a carrier of bat rabies because of its migratory habits, but fortunately it has not as yet been incriminated in Canada. Perhaps its solitary behaviour lessens the risk of contact with other carriers. In any event its arboreal habits seldom bring it into contact with humans.

Evening Bat (*Nycticeius humeralis humeralis*)
A single specimen of the evening bat taken by William Saunders at Point Pelee on May 16, 1911, is the only known record of this species in Canada. It is in the collection of the Royal Ontario Museum in Toronto.

The evening bat, which looks superficially like a miniature big brown bat with a darker brown fur and buffy under parts, lives in small colonies. It hides in hollow trees and church steeples and behind shutters. Cultivated and natural clearings in the southeastern hardwood forests of the United States are the natural habitats of the evening bats; its habits in Canada are unknown.

Hoary Bat (*Lasiurus cinereus*)
The hoary bat is the largest bat species in Canada. It measures almost six inches (15 cm) in length. The fur is long, dense and silky. This is a migratory species that is not found at Point Pelee during the summer months. The hoary bat's preferred habitat is the coniferous forest areas.

Hares and rabbits (Order *Lagomorpha*)

European Hare (*Lepus europaeus*)
Introduced from Germany in 1912 near Brantford, Ontario, the European hare (erroneously referred to as a jackrabbit) has since become common in southern Ontario.

Two sight records were made in the park during the 1974 deer drive. This species prefers open fields and pastures near woodlots. With old fields returning to their natural state in the park area, it is doubtful whether this hare will become a significant part of the park fauna.

Eastern Cottontail Rabbit (*Sylvilagus floridanus*)
At Point Pelee the cottontail is found in old fields and in low cover, such as along the transition areas between marsh and

forest, and beach and forest. In summer the cottontail feeds on grasses, herbs and leaves of shrubs, and in winter on twigs, bark and winter buds.

As a common victim of the coyote, red fox, long-tailed weasel, mink, owls and hawks, the cottontail rabbit is extremely important in the food chain.

Rodents (Order *Rodentia*)

Eastern Grey Squirrel (*Sciurus carolinensis*)
The eastern grey squirrel is a common resident of Point Pelee National Park with both black and grey phases being represented in approximately equal numbers.

This is a squirrel of the hardwood forest, where it forages on the ground for fallen nuts, berries, insects and other invertebrates, and fungi. It is often seen feeding on buds and young leaves in the tree tops in early spring. Nests are often visible as leafy masses in trees and branches.

Eastern Fox Squirrel (*Sciurus niger*)
Although the distribution of the eastern fox squirrel extends to the southern boundary of Ontario, this species is established

Eastern Fox Squirrel

Red Fox

MAMMALS

Cottontail Rabbit

only on Pelee Island, about eight-and-a-half miles southwest of the mainland, where it was introduced from Ohio around 1890.

Fox squirrels are now common in the drier, wooded areas of Pelee Island. They were also introduced into Point Pelee where they thrived at first, but they were decimated by excessive hunting around 1925. However, fox squirrels were re-introduced into Southern Ontario in 1969 and 1970, and one was sighted at Point Pelee in May 1977.

The fox squirrel is a large, diurnal tree squirrel, larger than the grey squirrel. As with the grey squirrel, there are at least three well-marked colour phases: red, black and grey, as well as combinations of these. Each phase is, however, somewhat different from the equivalent phase in the grey squirrel. It is hunted on Pelee Island during the autumn.

Strangely enough, the red squirrel (*Tamiasciurus hudsonicus*) has not been recorded at Point Pelee for some time and may have been extirpated. The woodchuck (*Marmota monax*) is uncommon in the park, but burrows were noted and an individual sighted in May, 1977. There are no recent records for the eastern flying squirrel (*Glaucomys volans*) and this species is now

Grey Squirrel

MAMMALS

thought to be extinct in the park. A thorough study would establish the status of this group of animals in Point Pelee National Park. The beaver (*Castor canadensis*) is no longer an inhabitant of the park area but was apparently present at Point Pelee in prehistoric times, since skeletal remains were found at archaeological digs in the park.

Baird's deer mouse inhabits the dry open grassland areas of the park. The woodland deer mouse may be present in the wooded areas, but there are no recent records of this species. The white-footed mouse is common in most areas of Point Pelee. It was found to be the most abundant mouse in a census taken in midsummer of 1971. The meadow vole, common in grasslands, was second in abundance. During the same survey, one meadow jumping mouse was caught in a wet marsh border area.

Possibly further studies will reveal the presence of the pine vole (*Pitymys pinetorum*), a Carolinian species which in Canada occurs only in the area immediately to the north of Lake Erie. Contrary to its name, the pine vole prefers hardwood forest with substantial ground cover.

Striped Skunk

The Norway rat (*Rattus norvegicus*), recorded at Point Pelee in 1907, has not been seen recently. It is not considered a desirable species. Mice and voles are important prey animals of coyote, red fox, weasels, hawks, owls and snakes, and also provide food for migratory birds of prey.

Baird's Deer Mouse (*Peromyscus maniculatus bairdii*)
The prairie or Baird's deer mouse is a small, light-coloured subspecies of the common deer mouse. It has a limited distribution in Canada, where it inhabits fields, plains and beaches in southern Manitoba and southern Ontario.

This race invaded southwestern Ontario prior to 1907, no doubt from southern Michigan, and spread rapidly northeastwards along the shores of Lakes Erie and Ontario. At Point Pelee, Baird's deer mouse is usually found along the open grassy areas of beaches and lightly wooded areas.

Woodland Deer Mouse (*Peromyscus maniculatus gracilis*)
The woodland deer mouse usually prefers shady forests and avoids open areas. Seeds comprise a great part of its diet, although it also eats insects, other invertebrates and small fruits.

White-Footed Mouse (*Peromyscus leucopus nove boraceusis*)
The white-footed mouse is the most abundant mouse species in the park. It frequents forests and the border areas of woodland and field. Its food preferences are much the same as those of the woodland deer mouse.

Meadow Vole (*Microtus pennsylvanicus*)
Meadow voles are commonly encountered at Point Pelee, since they frequent readily accessible old fields and colonized beach areas. Because of their substantial numbers, they are an important food source for snakes, birds of prey and carnivorous mammals. The bulk of their diet consists of grasses and sedges.

Muskrat (*Ondatra zibethicus*)
Another important rodent of Point Pelee, abundant in the marshes, is the muskrat whose conical house, made of cattails, is readily apparent.

From a two-year study conducted at Point Pelee in 1969 and 1970, it was learned that the muskrat population may fluctuate from year to year, depending on the water level in the marshes. In years of high summer waters, determined in part by Lake Erie levels, the muskrat may be especially abundant. Low water levels prior to 1965 corresponded to a decline in the muskrat population; but in 1965 the water of the marshes began to rise and with it the muskrat population. The year 1969 was a peak

MAMMALS 63

Racoon

Muskrat

year, and was followed by a decline from which the muskrat population has still not fully recovered.

The food of the muskrat commonly consists of cattail, spadderdock roots and water lilies, along with some animal matter, such as crustaceans. In the past, muskrats were an important source of food for Indian hunters and settlers. Muskrat trapping by local residents was permitted until 1959, and even today poaching is sometimes a problem.

The muskrat's chief predators at Point Pelee are mink, raccoons, hawks and owls, with the young being especially vulnerable.

Meadow Jumping Mouse (*Zapus hudsonius*)
The jumping mouse is seldom seen at Point Pelee, as it prefers damp field areas and is noctural in habit. Winter is spent in hibernation. The bulk of the jumping mouse's diet consists of grasses and fleshy fruit.

Carnivores (Order *Carnivora*)

Coyote (*Canis latrans*)
Within the present century the coyote has spread eastward from northwestern Ontario through the province and into western Quebec. Coyotes are known to be residents of Point Pelee and are often heard howling after dark, but because of their wary nature they are rarely seen.

During a study to determine the status of the coyote in the park three empty dens with fresh scats were located at the entrance to one den. From scat examination it appears that rabbits are the most important coyote food, with voles, birds, eggs, frogs and carrion also being eaten. Coyotes also eat large insects such as grasshoppers and crickets, as well as fruit and berries.

Attacks on livestock and other animals attributed to coyotes are frequently found to be the work of wild dogs. There is no evidence that coyotes prey on deer in the park.

Grey Fox (*Urocyon cinereoargenteus*)
The grey fox is another predator which is currently extending its range into Ontario and Quebec. Three separate localities are known for this species in southern Ontario: along the north shore of Lake Erie, on the north shore of Lake Ontario east of Durham County, and in the Rainy River district.

This species has been recorded on the Point and may be present in the park. But since it dens in hollow logs or trees, and evades its pursuers by climbing to the top of trees, it is not easy to detect and it has not been recorded in recent years.

Red Fox (*Vulpes vulpes*)

A very small, possibly transient population of red fox is found in the park, where its dens have been discovered on several occasions. Cottontail rabbits and meadow voles are probably its chief prey at Point Pelee.

Raccoon (*Procyon lotor*)

The raccoon is very common at Point Pelee. It is a frequent nocturnal predator, feeding on frogs, turtle eggs and occasionally turtles, young muskrats and a variety of invertebrates. Small birds, mammals and vegetable matter are also included in the diet.

These animals are perhaps most frequently seen in the vicinity of the marsh, and are often observed on the boardwalk on summer evenings. Raccoons are not particularly shy, and for this reason are encouraged by park visitors who either feed them directly or leave garbage for them. The resulting large

Mink

population of raccoons may present a threat to certain turtle species such as the endangered spotted turtle.

Short-Tailed Weasel (*Mustela erminea*)
The ermine or short-tailed weasel has been recorded at Point Pelee, although not frequently, for it is essentially a more northern species. It has been observed in the woodlands and old fields where it preys on mice, rabbits, birds and amphibians.

Long-Tailed Weasel (*Mustela frenata*)
Long-tailed weasels are a more common species in the park, particularly in the woodland areas. However, it is not uncommon to see this weasel in fields and around the border of the marsh, either by day or night. Mice, small reptiles, small birds and rabbits, fall prey to this voracious little predator.

Mink (*Mustela vison*)
The mink, larger than either the ermine or long-tailed weasel, is found in and around the marsh, and specimens may occasionally be seen on the boardwalk in spring and early summer. These animals are agile predators both on land and in the water, where they hunt for invertebrates, fish, frogs, snakes, birds and small mammals, including muskrat and rabbits.

Skunk (*Mephitis mephitis*)
By reputation alone, the skunk is one of the most widely known mammals. At Point Pelee the skunk is rare, and is smelled more often than it is seen. Skunks are omnivorous, feeding on assorted plants and animal matter. The bulk of their diet is insects, particularly larger beetles and grubs, and as such they are of great benefit to agriculturalists. This animal may also be a factor in the decline of the spotted turtle in the park.

The badger (*Taxidea taxus*) is present in southern Ontario along the north shore of Lake Erie, but has not yet been recorded in Point Pelee.

The otter (*Lutra canadensis*) also has not been seen in the park, but may from time to time be present in the marsh where fish, reptiles, amphibians, waterfowl and small mammals would comprise its diet.

Deer and elk (Order *Artiodactyla*)
Wapiti or American Elk (*Cervus canadensis*)
Until early in the history of settlement in Canada, the wapiti was found in southern Ontario. Skeletal remains have been found in archeological digs in the park. By 1850 wapiti had disappeared from eastern Canada, victims of hunters and of the destruction

of their forest habitat. This subspecies, *Cervus canadensis canadensis*, eventually became totally extinct.

Virginia or Whitetail Deer (*Odocoileus virginianus*)
The whitetail deer was reportedly abundant at Point Pelee before the settlers came. Its numbers were drastically reduced by hunting and habitat destruction. More deer were reintroduced into the park in 1941. Thirty-five animals were recorded during a 1974 deer drive, but the estimated reproduction rate is low. The distribution of deer in the park is related to their seasonal food preferences. In summer, heavy use is made of abandoned farmland, while in fall the deer also use shrub areas. In winter, deer range more widely over the park but show a preference for the red cedar and shrub areas.

Reptiles
&
Amphibians

Point Pelee, despite its small size and heavy human use, supports a large and varied population of reptiles and amphibians. Since 1895, thirty species and subspecies of reptiles and amphibians have been recorded for the park, comprising the following: 1 skink, 10 snakes, 8 turtles, 2 salamanders, 2 toads and 7 frogs. The lower Great Lakes-St Lawrence Valley region has a diverse population of these animals, more so than any other part of Canada. Many of the species found at Point Pelee are also found at Georgian Bay Islands National Park and St Lawrence National Park.

There are several species of reptiles and amphibians with ranges that include the Point Pelee area, which have not been found in the park. For the most part, the park does not offer suitable living conditions for these animals. It may also be the case that the isolated situation of Point Pelee, bounded by farmland and the lake, prevents natural invasion.

Some amphibians and reptiles, however, that were once found in the park have vanished over the years. These animals, like all other living things, have particular requirements of their environment. If these life requirements can no longer be met, then they will no longer be successful in that environment. Changes in Point Pelee, such as aging of the marsh and forest and a natural regeneration of old fields, may be reason enough to cause change. When the populations fall to very low numbers, the isolated nature of the park inhibits a replenishment.

The most recent survey of reptiles and amphibians in the park, conducted in 1972, yielded 18 species. One of these, the eastern box turtle, was new both to the park and to Canada, and its arrival is still a mystery.

A formerly abundant turtle species which is presently losing ground is the attractive spotted turtle, a species numbered among Canada's endangered reptiles. Other turtle species resident in the park such as the snapping turtle, Midland painted turtle and Blanding's turtle are faring quite well and appear to have healthy breeding populations. The stinkpot, or musk turtle, and the map turtle are also present, but are considered uncommon in the park.

Frogs and toads, especially the American toad, green frog, northern leopard frog and bullfrog have withstood human pressure in the park quite successfully. Northern spring peepers are not so common but are believed to be breeding successfully. Fowler's toad and the eastern grey treefrog, both recorded before the 1972 survey but not encountered at that time, may still be present. Blanchard's cricket frog, thought to be extinct at Point Pelee, was heard calling in May during the 1972 survey.

Snakes, however, have lost heavily in numbers and in species over the years. Long persecuted by man, only four species remain of the ten that have been recorded in the park. One of these, the eastern fox snake, although common in the park, is on the Canadian endangered species list.

The six snakes no longer found at Point Pelee are: the timber rattlesnake, believed extinct in Canada; the eastern massasauga rattlesnake, occurring locally within its range but much reduced in numbers; the harmless eastern hognose snake; the blue racer; and the black rat snake. These five species are all large, and either rare or endangered in Canada. The sixth species, the eastern milk snake, is a smaller snake that frequents open dry areas.

All of these snakes are terrestrial and have been threatened by man in the areas of heaviest human use, such as the beaches, dry woods and fields. The elusive northern brown snake (DeKay's snake), northern water snake and eastern garter snake seem to be breeding successfully, little disturbed by the presence of man. The success of the northern brown snake is probably due to its small size and secretive nature. The northern water snake and eastern garter snake are probably thriving because they do not rely on a terrestrial habitat.

One species of lizard, the five-lined skink, is a common park inhabitant. A single specimen of the eastern tiger salamander, reported for Point Pelee in 1915, has not been seen since that time. Since other more common salamanders are not present in the park, it is likely that Point Pelee does not afford a suitable habitat.

A list of reptiles and amphibians that have been reported for Point Pelee National Park follows, with notes on their habits.

Amphibians
Mudpuppy (*Necturus maculosus*)
The mudpuppy lives in permanent bodies of fresh water. The belief that these animals can bark gives them their name. They eat aquatic animals of almost any size and they breath with gills, even as adults. The size and bushiness of the gills reflect the type of water in which they live – foul or clear, warm or cool.
Eastern Tiger Salamander (*Ambystoma tigrinum tigrinum*)
The eastern tiger salamander has been recorded only once in

Canada – at Point Pelee on October 2, 1915, by P.A. Taverner. More recent attempts to confirm its existence in this country have failed.

This species has been known to reach the imposing length of slightly over 13 inches (33 cm), although its average size is somewhat less. It gets its name from its characteristic colour pattern – yellow blotches on a dark background.

American Toad (*Bufo americanus*)
The American toad is a very common species all over Ontario northward to latitude 55°, and is the most common toad found in the park area. The colour of this species is exceedingly variable, usually some hue of brown, marbled and blotched with dark and light markings. It may reach four inches (10 cm) in length.

The moist Point Pelee woods, with an abundance of insects, provide a good habitat for this amphibian. During the month of July, numerous young toads may be encountered.

Fowler's Toad (*Bufo woodhousei fowleri*)
Fowler's toad is found in southern Ontario along the beaches of Lake Ontario, although it is very rare, if not extinct, at Point Pelee. It has not been seen in the park for several years despite careful searches by the park staff. However, on Pelee Island, Long Point and a few other lower Great Lakes locales Fowler's toads still hop around in fair numbers.

The Fowler's toad is easily mistaken for the American toad, but differs from that species by being generally smaller and slightly greenish in colour. It has a different voice and breeds a little later than the more common species. Fowler's toad is an essentially southern amphibian reaching the northern limit of its range in southern Ontario.

Blanchard's Cricket Frog (*Acris crepitans blanchardi*)
Point Pelee and Pelee Island are the only known Canadian homes of Blanchard's cricket frog. One specimen was found in the park in 1920 and more were subsequently located on Pelee Island. No other specimens have been taken at Point Pelee since that time, and the species was believed to have become extinct in the park until a specimen was heard calling in May, 1972.

Blanchard's cricket frog has tiny disks on its toes and fully webbed feet. It varies in colour from brown to olive-green, with a varied pattern of dark blotches and streaks. It frequents marshes and edges of ponds and does not climb like other tree-frogs. Its call, which is uttered intermittently, sounds something

Tree Frog

like the tapping of two pebbles, and has considerable carrying power.

Spring Peeper (*Hyla crucifer*)
The spring peeper, found commonly throughout much of eastern Canada, is characterized by an x mark across its back. This species should be watched for in the woods, either on the ground or perched on plants along the edge of the old shoreline ditches. They are more likely to be heard than seen, especially in the month of May, when they call with their characteristic peeps to attract mates.

Eastern Grey Treefrog (*Hyla versicolor versicolor*)
The eastern grey treefrog will most likely be heard before it is seen, for it can camouflage itself by changing its skin colour to match its surroundings. As their name suggests, these frogs are usually found foraging on insects in trees throughout the year, except during the mating season, when they go to the ponds to spawn.

Western Chorus Frog (*Pseudacris triseriata triseriata*)
This small terrestrial frog likes woods or open areas with enough vegetation to preserve moisture. It seems to favour small temporary ponds for spawning. Although it is usually found in prairie areas, this frog seems to have taken to agricultural areas in the park. This may explain the presence of the

western chorus frog near the north park boundary and in the farmland beyond the park.

Bullfrog (*Rana catesbeiana*)

The bullfrog, largest of eastern Northern American frogs, sometimes attains a length of over seven inches (18 cm). It frequents larger bodies of water, and is quite common in the Point Pelee marsh. This species eats a variety of animals – other frogs, fish, turtles, small snakes, birds, mice and insects. In turn it is considered a delicacy by many people. The characteristic deep 'jug-a-rum' call of the bullfrog may be heard in the spring and early summer.

Green Frog (*Rana clamitans melanota*)

The green frog is sometimes mistaken for the bullfrog but it is somewhat smaller, ranging from three to four inches (7 to 10 cm). Like the bullfrog, it is decidedly an aquatic animal. The croak of this frog, sounding like a loose banjo string, is heard at spawning time, during late May to July.

Northern Leopard Frog (*Rana pipiens pipiens*)

The leopard frog, readily identified by its dark spots on a green or brown background, is the most common frog at Point Pelee.

Spotted Turtle

This species is to be found in aquatic areas, but it is also known as the 'meadow frog' because of its habit of wandering into meadows some distance from the water to search for insects.

Reptiles

Common Snapping Turtle (*Chelydra serpentina serpentina*)
The common snapping turtle is the most widely distributed turtle in North America, and the largest turtle found in the Point Pelee marsh.

These antedeluvian reptiles are usually seen in late July when females come out to lay their eggs. The rest of the year they spend much time foraging on the marsh bottom for dead, but not rotting, fish or other small animals and vegetation. The name accurately describes their disposition.

Common Musk Turtle (*Sternotherus odoratus*)
The common musk turtle, or stinkpot, gets its name from four glands which emit, as protection, an unpleasant odour when the turtle is picked up. Like the snapping turtle, it is pugnacious. Musk turtles are carnivorous and forage on the bottom of the marsh for carrion, insects and other small animals. The stinkpot is not common at Point Pelee.

Spotted Turtle (*Clemmys guttata*)
The spotted turtle is a small, friendly and beautiful turtle which has been reduced in numbers at Point Pelee. Only one individual was reported during the 1972 survey, whereas in 1920 it was a common member of the park's fauna.

These turtles are about five inches (13 cm) long and favour pond or marsh areas like the Point Pelee marsh where there is a muddy bottom. Habitat changes are probably the main cause of the decrease in the number of spotted turtles at Point Pelee, and in southern Ontario generally.

Eastern Box Turtle (*Terrapene carolina carolina*)
Although the eastern box turtle's normal range does not extend into Point Pelee, several have been found in the park in the last decade, with eight being reported in 1972. Point Pelee, with its moist woods offers a good habitat for this mainly terrestrial reptile. Either Point Pelee has become an extension of the box turtle's range, or people have been, ill-advisedly, releasing their pets in the park.

Three individuals were tagged during the 1972 survey, and it will be interesting to see if, in future surveys, the eastern box turtle has established itself at Point Pelee National Park.

Blanding's Turtle (*Emydoidea blandingi*)
Blanding's turtle is quite common at Point Pelee where it is easily identified by its bright yellow chin. A hinge on the undershell allows it to partially close its shell. These turtles are essentially aquatic but will wander on land and are more readily found in the park during the breeding season in late June. Blanding's turtle is an omnivorous feeder both in water and on land.

Eastern Spiny Softshell Turtle (*Trionyx spiniferus spiniferus*)
The eastern spiny softshell turtle is an odd-looking animal which is often referred to as 'pancake' or 'flapjack' because of the unusual shape and texture of the shell. These animals lack the usual hard protective upper shell or carapace which is characteristic of other turtles.

In Canada, this species is confined to southern Ontario and to southern Quebec, where its population is declining rapidly because of spreading urban development. Formerly, softshell turtles were sometimes caught in the fishermen's nets at Point Pelee. It seemed they lived in the water and came on to the beach only to lay their eggs. Crayfish and insects constitute the bulk of this species' diet.

Common Map Turtle (*Graptemys geographica*)
Map turtles are one of the larger turtle species at Point Pelee National Park. Their maximum size is close to eleven inches (28 cm) in the female, but only six to seven inches (15 cm to 17.5 cm) in the male. Their large jaws are well suited for crunching snails and crayfish, the bulk of their diet. These turtles get their name from their carapace (upper shell) pattern, which resembles a topographical map of light lines on a dark background. This species is considered to be uncommon in the park.

Midland Painted Turtle (*Chrysemys picta marginata*)
Painted turtles are the most common turtles in the park. They can frequently be seen on any hot summer day sunning themselves in the marsh area. These omnivorous turtles comprise four subspecies of North American painted turtles, so named because of red markings around the edge of the shell and a yellow stripe on the neck. A black patch on the undershell distinguishes the Midland painted turtle from the other races.

Five-Lined Skink (*Eumeces fasciatus*)
The five-lined skink, the only lizard found in eastern Canada, lives in the rotting logs in the moist Point Pelee woodlands, and along the east beach.

Less than nine inches (23 cm) long, it is an agile creature, quick to elude its enemies. Should it be confronted by a predator, however, nature has given the skink a safety mechanism – a detachable tail that breaks off near the base. Within six to ten months a shorter tail will have taken its place, and the skink will be none the worse for its experience.

The eggs are laid in the early summer, and the female skink protects her brood throughout the incubation period. Young animals have a characteristic blue tail, the source of the alternate name 'blue-tailed skink'. The animal's food consists of insects, larvae, earthworms and other small invertebrates, and some small vertebrates. In Canada, the five-lined skink is confined to southern Ontario.

Eastern Garter Snake (*Thamnophis sirtalis sirtalis*)
This is one of the most common and familiar snakes, easily recognised by its three stripes on a black or dark background. These snakes inhabit damp woods, fields and marshes, and range over a large part of eastern North America. They prey on a wide variety of animals, from insects to small mammals.

At Point Pelee (and Long Point) eastern garter snakes show a tendency to produce melanistic individuals: the skin becomes an unusual black colour. With the exception of white lower jaws and throat, the adults are coal black and might pass for small black rat snakes.

Eastern Spiny Softshelled Turtle

Black Rat Snake (*Elaphe obsoleta obsoleta*)
The black rat snake, or pilot snake, is the largest of Canadian snakes, occasionally reaching eight feet (244 cm) in length. Rat snakes prey on mice, young rats and small birds, which they constrict in their strong coils.

Unfortunately, this species has become rare or non-existent at Point Pelee, and it has not been recorded in the park in recent years.

Eastern Fox Snake (*Elaphe vulpina gloydi*)
The eastern fox snake was formerly more common at Point Pelee than it is today. In Canada, this handsome snake is found only in southwestern Ontario and along the shores of Georgian Bay.

This species is readily identified by its dark brown spots on a yellow-brown background. The head is a coppery colour. Like various other harmless snakes, the eastern fox snake vibrates its tail when it is alarmed, so it is sometimes called the 'hardwood rattler' and is erroneously believed to be venomous.

The eastern fox snake is essentially a water species, never found far from marshes, ponds and shorelines, where it preys on rodents, small mammals, birds and their eggs. Like its close relative, the black rat snake, it is also a constrictor. In favourable habitats it is not uncommon to observe this snake basking on mats of dead reeds that border small bodies of water.

A special study has been in progress since 1967 to determine the status and habits of the eastern fox snake at Point Pelee. Unfortunately visitors kill many of these snakes on the roads and elsewhere in the park. This study and the park's interpretive programme should do much to develop a better conservation attitude by the public towards this and other snakes.

Blue Racer (*Coluber constrictor foxi*)
The blue racer is confined in Canada solely to Huron and Essex Counties in southern Ontario. It is an attractive snake, slender, bluish-green above with a greenish-white or yellowish belly, and may exceed a length of six feet (183 cm).

This species was found at Point Pelee in the early 1900s but as with many of the Park's snakes, it has disappeared from the area. There are records of fifteen or sixteen blue racers having been found in 1913 and for some years following in Essex County, including Point Pelee. One of these, taken in the park on November 2, 1915, measured six feet, three inches (190 cm) in length. The prey of this species consists chiefly of rodents, reptiles, amphibians and insects.

Eastern Hognose Snake

Eastern Milk Snake (*Lampropeltis triangulum tirangulum*)
The milk snake is a beautiful, slender species with black bordered red-brown blotches on a light or greyish ground colour. It feeds largely on rodents which it hunts in woodlands or farmland clearings. As a member of the king snake family, it probably also preys on venomous snakes. The eastern milk snake, regrettably, is another native snake of Point Pelee National Park that has been depleted, and may be extinct in the park.
DeKay's Snake (*Storeria dekayi dekayi*)
This snake, also known as the northern brown snake, is a small species, usually nine to thirteen inches (23 cm to 33 cm) long, that feeds on small invertebrates, and possibly on vertebrates such as small frogs. At Point Pelee, these snakes have been depleted in number but appear to be making a comeback. Their natural habitats include marsh and most wooded areas.
Eastern Hognose Snake (*Heterodon platyrhinos*)
Hognose snakes were once common on sandy, sparsely timbered areas of Point Pelee, where colour phases varying from yellow with dark brown markings to almost black were represented. This is another species whose Canadian range is restricted to southern Ontario. This species has probably become

extinct in the park area, as no specimens have been discovered there for some time.

This snake is well-known for its habit of rearing up to hiss and spread its head when approached. It will roll over and play dead if the initial bluff fails. Such antics, doubtless, are frightening to the passer-by who fears that he has come upon a rattlesnake, or other highly dangerous snake. Consequently, many hognose snakes have been wantonly slaughtered. Hognose snakes prey chiefly on toads and frogs, especially the former.

Northern Water Snake (*Natrix sipedon sipedon*)

The northern water snake lives in a variety of habitats. At Point Pelee, it is usually found in marsh areas. It preys on fish, frogs and sometimes on small mammals. This species has a series of grey-brown bands on its grey back, but in some older specimens the colouration may be so dark as to eliminate the pattern.

A pale race of this species, the Lake Erie water snake (*Natrix sipedon insularum*), in which the pattern is usually lacking, is found isolated on the Lake Erie islands.

Eastern Massasauga Rattlesnake (*Sistrurus catenatus catenatus*)

Park visitors have little chance of meeting a massasauga rattlesnake at Point Pelee, since this species was last reported in the park area in 1895! Many massasauga rattlesnakes were probably eaten by pigs belonging to the park's early settlers, and people also killed this snake. The ideal habitat still exists for them at Point Pelee, and rattlesnakes are still to be found in some local communities, notably in the LaSalle area west of Windsor.

Timber Rattlesnake (*Crotalus horridus horridus*)

The timber rattlesnake has not been recorded in Ontario since 1941, and may be extinct in this country. Only one specimen of this large, venomous snake has been found at Point Pelee, and that was near the tip of the Point on September 29, 1918. The capture of a young individual might indicate that there were others near by, but as this specimen was an adult measuring four feet eight inches (142 cm) in length, it could have arrived at the Point by swimming across the lake. At Point Pelee, as in many other localities in southern Ontario, rattlesnakes have long since been exterminated.

Fish

The diversity and abundance of fish in Lake Erie is naturally great because of the lake's southerly position, river connections and high productivity levels. Commercial fisheries were established soon after settlement and yielded large catches of herring, whitefish and lake trout (*Salvelinus namaycush*). Decreases in these fisheries are well documented and have been related to over-exploitation and to the introduction of sea lamprey (*Petromyzon marinus*). The decline in numbers has also occurred with less common fish, some of which are now extreme rarities. These include sturgeons (*Acipenser fulvescens*), blueback herring (*Alosa aestivalis*) and some ciscos (*Coregonus spp*). At the time of early settlement, muskellunge (*Esox masquinongy*), northern pike (*Esox lucius*), lake whitefish (*Coregonus clupeaformis*), walleye (*Stizostedion vitreum*), sauger (*S. canadense*), lake herring (*Coregonus artedii*), bass and several species of catfish were all frequently caught. Various southern gars and bowfins were abundant.

At Point Pelee this diversity is reduced, since the available fish habitat is confined to several shallow, reedy ponds with only restricted access to western Lake Erie. In summer, rapidly rising water temperatures preclude the establishment of cold or deep water fish.

The fish that live here reflect the restriction of habitat, and most species found are tolerant of warm water conditions. The most abundant species are: bowfin (*Amia calva*), northern pike (*Esox lucius*), carp (*Cyprinus carpio*), brown bullhead (*Ameiurus nebulosus*), perch (*Perca flavescens*), pumpkinseed (*Lepomis gibbosus*) and bluegill (*L. macrochirus*). Carp (*Cyprinus carpio*) and goldfish (*Carassius auratus*) have both been introduced to the park and now often reach large populations. In good years they appear to increase rapidly. There has been considerable interest by early season park visitors in smelt (*Osmerus mordax*) fishing. Large numbers of these fish congregate off the sandbanks to spawn.

Zoogeographically, Point Pelee is regarded as an important fish habitat where several species of southern or other affinity can be found. The Point supports a large variety of these species, including some of restricted range such as the lake chubsucker (*Erimyzon sucetta*), a rare fish known only from the marsh ponds of Point Pelee, Long Point, Rondeau and Lake St Clair. The golden redhorse (*Moxostoma erytrhrurum*) occurs only in western Lake Erie and southern Lake Huron, but others

FISH

Marsh Panorama

such as the silver redhorse (*M. anisurum*), which is also found at Point Pelee, are more widely distributed. Many other fish species with southerly ranges are found in the park but may be present, though rare, farther north. An example is the gizzard shad (*Dorosoma cepedianum*), which is close to the northern limit of its range at Point Pelee.

Brook silverside (*Labidesthes sicculus*) and the blackchin and blacknose shiners (*Notropis heterodon*), (*N. heterolepis*) are found in clear, weedy lakes and are becoming more rare or extirpated in many areas because of poor water quality. The grass pickerel (*Esox americanus vermiculatus*), a rare species, is occasionally found. It is present in isolated populations as far north as the Muskoka region.

Of great interest from the evolutionary point of view are the bowfin and gars which are living representatives of an ancient fossil fish order of the Jurassic age. They may be regarded as 'living fossils'. All are predators, and the bowfin is especially abundant in the park. The spotted gar (*Lepisosteus oculatus*), which occurs rarely in western Lake Erie, may be found in Canada, only at Point Pelee and in parts of Lake St Clair. The longnose gar (*Lepisosteus osseus*) is more common and there is evidence from middens (mounds of refuse left by the Indians), that they used this species as a source of food.

Insects

Monarch Butterfly

INSECTS

Insects far exceed all other terrestrial animals in number. Their short life span and great numbers per generation have allowed them to adapt, by evolutionary trial and error, to practically all the world's environments. Several hundred thousand species have been described thus far, more than three times the number of species in the remainder of the animal kingdom. Populations often reach millions per acre.

Insects exhibit a seemingly endless variety of forms and structures to adapt to living conditions. Their shapes range from the picturesque to the grotesque. All are intricately involved in the life processes of the world.

As is the case with other groups, the insects at Point Pelee include many southern species rare in Canada. Undoubtedly, the list will be lengthened by future investigations, for the insects have not yet attracted the many dedicated observers that the birds have. The keenest surveys have been undertaken by lepidopterists who were aware of the potential of Point Pelee at least as early as 1882, but published accounts have been few and much information and many collections have been lost to the public.

William Saunders was the first to write of insects at Point Pelee, following his visits in the summer of 1882. He was impressed by the numbers of dragonflies he had seen cruising over marshes, fields and beaches. Later E.M. Walker, working at the Royal Ontario Museum in Toronto, collected insects at Point Pelee. His records from that area were published in the 'First List of Ontario Odonata'. Saunders reported in the *Canadian Entomologist* for 1883 his first encounter with the giant swallowtail and the very local olive hairstreak butterflies. He also made reference to finding at Point Pelee the Mexican sulphur (*Eurema mexicana*), an extremely rare visitor to Canada.

Percy Taverner, during collecting trips to Point Pelee from 1908 to 1919, recorded his sugaring activities (a process of collecting moths by luring them to a sweet and intoxicating substance painted on tree trunks – usually a combination of molasses, brown sugar and beer.):

> 'That night we sugared the woods across the road from the campgrounds for moths with considerable luck. The first round of sugared route we found underwings *Catocala spp.* on nearly every tree and took five species. *Catocala cara* was the commonest species but so far I have made out *C. grynea* and *C. cerogama* among the spoils.'

In all, Taverner collected 12 Catocala species: *C. cara, cerogama, parta, grynea, habilis, vidua, piatrix, unijuga, amica, concumbens, relicta* and *amatrix.*

Rare southern migrant butterflies that may be seen at Point Pelee include the snout butterfly (*Libythea bachmannii*), buckeye (*Precis coenia*), dogface (*Colias (Zerene) cesonia*), cloudless sulphur (*Phoebis sennae eubule*), and rarer still – the regal fritillary (*Speyeria idalia*), zebra swallowtail (*Papilio marcellus*) and the Mexican sulphur. These species, along with the black witch moth (*Erebus odora*), frequently end their northward journey across Lake Erie by being washed up on the shore along with debris. All these insects are summer immigrants from the south, apparently not able to overwinter in southern Ontario. A few have been observed flying southward in the fall, sometimes in the company of migrating monarchs.

Whether or not they can be termed truly migrational has yet to be determined. The term migration in its strictest sense denotes fairly continuous movement from one area to another with periodic return to the original area. However, in the case of insect migration, it is most frequently taken to mean oneway movement from one area to another with no return flight.

The monarch butterfly (*Danaus plexippus*) is the only North American insect proven to exhibit true migrational behaviour. Monarchs migrate through Point Pelee in the fall, some years in such abundance as to form clusters on trees and shrubs. On September 15, 1935 – a particularly good year – monarchs were observed leaving the Point at the net rate of forty-three per minute.

The monarch's range corresponds to that of the milkweed, which is the insect's food plant, and both can be seen over most of North America. Seasonally, though, these butterflies are more numerous in certain areas, as they spend the summer months and breed in the northern United States and southern Canada and migrate south in the late fall. Each spring and fall there is a movement of monarchs from one range to the other.

During their flight the monarchs reach speeds of thirty miles per hour. The longest recorded flight is more than 1,800 miles, from Ontario to Mexico. The fall migration is, of course, more spectacular, augmented as it is by a new generation of monarchs moving south. This phenomenon may be observed at Point Pelee each year in late September and early October. Great numbers enter the park and gather on trees at the very tip of the

Point before they cross Lake Erie. Their numbers build to a peak every five to seven years when the population reaches enormous proportions.

As previously mentioned, various insects from time to time fly in company with migrating monarchs. The giant swallowtail (*Papilio cresphontes*), spicebush swallowtail (*P. troilus*) and the wasp (*Polistes fuscatus pallipes*), together with the big green darner (dragonfly) (*Anax junius*), are among those which have been identified in such flights at Point Pelee. Other species of dragonflies, *Libellula puchella* and *Aeschno constricta*, and the red admiral (*Vanessa atalanta*) and European cabbage butterflies (*Pieris rapae*), have also exhibited migratory behaviour at Point Pelee, but in all cases migratory status is still to be determined.

Apart from the monarch butterfly, the study of the phenomenon of insect migration at Point Pelee has been largely neglected, probably in favour of the more spectacular bird migrations. Undoubtedly, however, Point Pelee has considerable potential as a research site for the study of insect migration.

The following species all have their stronghold in Point Pelee, and are either confined in Canada to the park area, or are found only very rarely elsewhere in southwestern and southern Ontario:

Monarch Butterfly

Butterflies (Order *Lepidoptera*)

The giant swallowtail butterfly (*Papilio cresphontes*), the largest butterfly species native to eastern North America, is a truly magnificent species, with bright yellow bands on a dark brown background. This species is found in Canada only in Point Pelee National Park and environs, although in the latter part of the nineteenth century it had a much wider range, as far north and east as Kingston, Ontario.

This butterfly is a reminder of the large, colourful butterflies of the tropics, from which this species undoubtedly originated; many very similar species are to be found throughout the New World tropics.

At Point Pelee, the caterpillar of the giant swallowtail feeds on the hop tree, which grows abundantly along the beach areas of the park. In some years, this swallowtail may not be uncommon at Point Pelee, but it is usually rare enough never to become commonplace. The giant swallowtail is best seen in the park during the month of August.

Another rare butterfly species of the park is the olive hairstreak (*Mitoura gryneus*). This species is extremely local in its distribution in this area because it is confined to its main host plant, the red cedar. It is a small species with a wingspread of a little over one inch (3 cm). The upper surface of the wings is largely two shades of brown, while the underside is greenish, adorned with various red and white stripes and spots. Apart from Point Pelee, the olive hairstreak is known only in two other Canadian localities, near Belleville and at Pinery Provincial Park in Ontario. This butterfly should be looked for in the park in late May and mid July.

The hackberry butterfly (*Asterocampa celtis*) and the tawny emperor (*A. clyton*) are two more species that are seldom seen in Canada outside of the park area. The hackberry butterfly is generally not uncommon in the park during July and August, and may be seen flying around the tops of hackberry trees. The tawny emperor, a rarer, and, as its name denotes, a more tawny-brown coloured butterfly, may be seen in company with the former species. Both are addicted to rotting fruit and excrement, a trait which collectors have used to their own advantage. While the butterflies are engrossed in their sticky repast they may be easily caught.

INSECTS 91

Hackberry Butterfly

Crickets, Grasshoppers, Katydids (Order *Orthoptera*)
The mole cricket (*Gryllotalpa hexadactyla*) is a small dark brown species about one inch (2.5 cm) long which burrows and makes tunnels in damp soil around the margins of streams and ponds. Sometimes the burrows may be six to eight inches (15 to 20 cm) deep. It not only burrows like a mole but its front legs, like those of the mole, are short and broad and adapted for digging. Mole crickets have wings and sometimes leave the burrow and fly about. They also sing or chirp like other crickets.

In Canada this species is found only in the southern portion of Essex County, Ontario, including Leamington and Point Pelee. Its general range is much farther south.

The seaside grasshopper (*Trimerotropis maritima interior*) is a short-horned species that looks like the ordinary grasshopper of our fields, except that its colour is very light grey to match the sandy soil where it lives. It inhabits the beaches and sandy cultivated fields near the shores of the Great Lakes. It is very abundant at Point Pelee, where it feeds on grasses and sedges, and sometimes it feeds on cultivated asparagus plants in the farmers' fields. It is active all day on the hot sand, whereas other creatures such as the ground beetle (*Geopinus*) or Fowler's toad have to burrow into the soil before daylight to survive in the same habitat.

In Canada, the northern katydid (*Pterophylla camellefolia*) is found only in the southern parts of Essex County, Ontario. This species is pale green with a conspicuous brown triangle on the wings. The body is about one and three-quarters inches (4.5 cm) long. The legs are long and the antennae very long.

This is the greatest singer of the insect world and one that really says its name, 'ka-ty-did'. It sings on warm nights from the dense foliage of oak, walnut and other trees. It is found from Point Pelee southward over most of the eastern United States.

Changing face of Point Pelee

Point Pelee from the air

The national park at Point Pelee was created in 1918 in an attempt to preserve this unique natural environment. Settlers, however, had already caused considerable changes at the Point. The establishment of the park could only reduce, but not eliminate, the continuing impact of human population and activity on the area.

At the same time, natural processes, slower and less obvious, continue to transform the Point.

A number of animals have disappeared from the Point Pelee area within the last two centuries. By the late 1800s and early 1900s bears, deer, prairie chicken, wild turkey, ruffed grouse and passenger pigeon had been eliminated by man from the peninsula. By the late 1950s blue pike, sauger, lake herring, sturgeon, lake whitefish and lake trout had become either extinct or significantly reduced in numbers in nearby Lake Erie, primarily as a result of human activity.

Some species have also been introduced to the Point Pelee area. Carp were apparently present in Lake Erie by about 1883, and smelt were reportedly introduced into the lake about 1932. In 1941, deer returned in limited numbers to Point Pelee.

With the arrival of French Canadian settlers in the early 1830s, domesticated European animals were introduced on the peninsula. During the 1800s and early 1900s cattle, horses, pigs and other animals were allowed to roam unrestricted throughout the natural reserve, browsing and grazing, with the flora of the peninsula providing free and suitable pasturage. However, in 1911, following critical comments by visitors about the large numbers of roaming cattle and hogs, widespread grazing of animals appears to have been substantially reduced. No references have been found to indicate that the uncontrolled grazing of domesticated animals continued later than 1918.

Much has been written in the past few years about the condition of the water of Lake Erie. Because of lake traffic, the fishing industry and development in the drainage basin of the Great Lakes, changes have occurred in plant and animal life. Population structures and communities, food resources, nutrient and species distribution are all affected.

In recent years there have been efforts to clean up the lake, and bacterial counts now appear to be at lower levels. However, it will likely be several years before appreciable changes take place, and the prospect of Lake Erie's ever reaching a pure state is extremely unlikely.

Much of the future of Point Pelee depends on the effects of erosion and flooding. As a shallow and warm lake, Erie is aging more rapidly than the other Great Lakes. In its aging process, Lake Erie is becoming rounder because of erosion around the shoreline. Slowly, but measurably, the surrounding land, depressed by the weight of the glaciers, is rebounding towards its original elevation. Estimates are that the water level of Lake Erie has been rising at a rate of 50 to 60 centimetres a century.

At Point Pelee particularly severe storm waves can sweep over the low beach ridges. Flooding, when it occurs, however, is generally brief, confined to the period of the storm. The vegetation growing just beyond the reach of the waves breaks the flow of wind, causing wind-blown sand to be dropped. Also, the plants anchor the sand in place by a mesh of stems and roots. Under extreme conditions, the vegetation can be torn loose. In these brief violent periods, the continual shoreline changes become much more obvious.

It should be remembered, however, that these processes have been going on for thousands of years, and that man has seen only a fraction of the continuous evolutionary process. Natural defences, sufficient for all but the most violent of conditions, are fortunately self-renewing.

Visiting Point Pelee

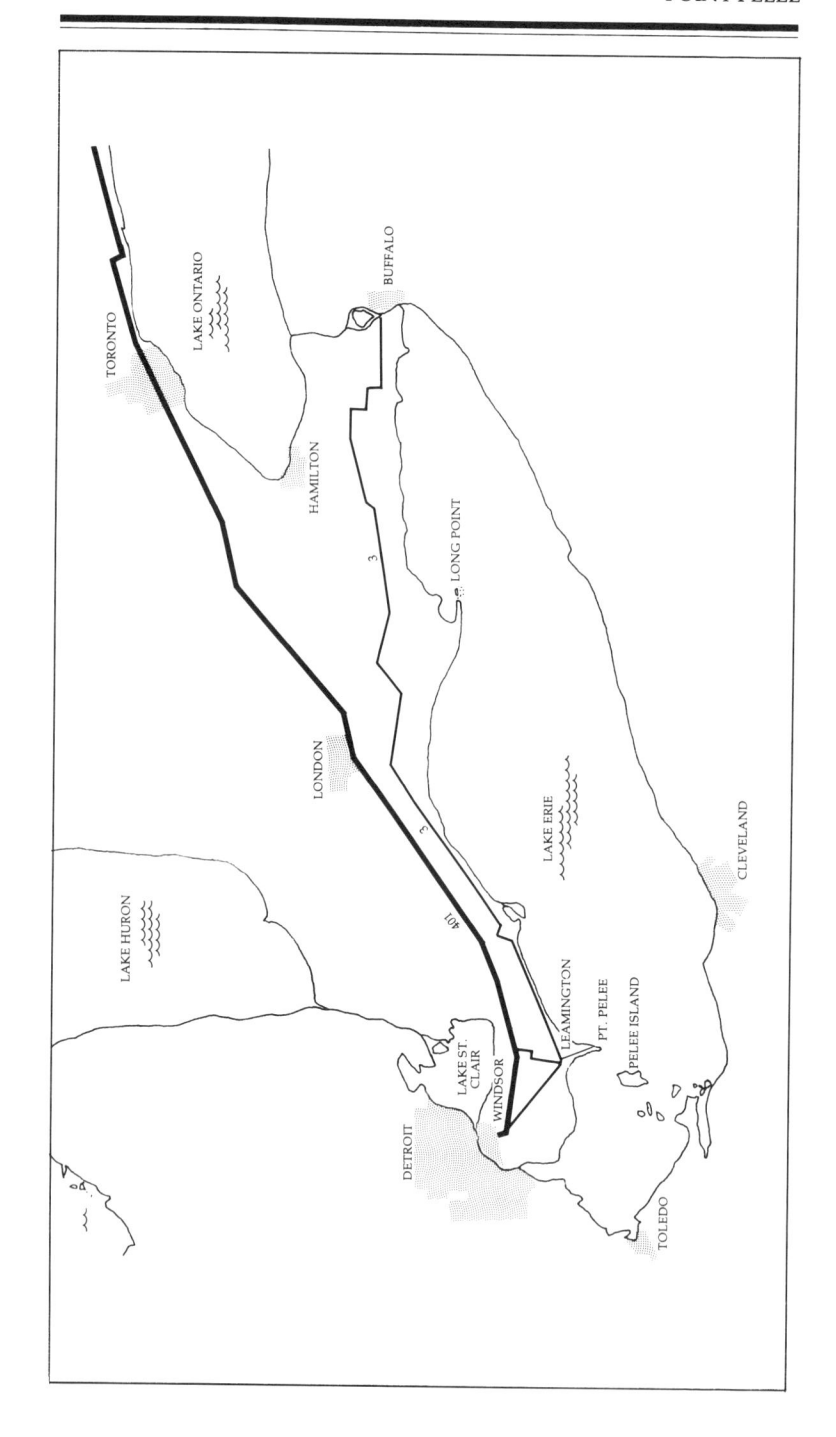

VISITING POINT PELEE

Point Pelee National Park is located in an extremely densely populated region. It is one of the most popular and most heavily used of Canada's 28 national parks. At the same time, it is one of the smallest parks in the system. This combination has created a number of problems, some of which haven't yet been solved.

For instance, vehicular traffic has had to be curtailed during the peak summer season, and replaced by a transit system, serving Black Willow, West and East Point beaches. These pollution-free trackless trains are equipped with a public address system to facilitate special interpretive programmes while passengers are en route. The trains operate daily, on designated routes between 9:00 a.m. and 9:00 p.m. from early April through Labour Day and during the weekends in September.

If you prefer, you can always reach any point in the park by foot. You are even able to cycle anywhere in the park, except the main highway. Walking is still the best and most popular way to see the park.

The Boardwalk Trail will lead you for more than a mile through the marshlands. A second nature trail, the Woodland Trail, begins at the Interpretive Centre. Other hiking trails are clearly marked and easy to reach.

Although camping is encouraged in most national parks, Point Pelee is too small and fragile to withstand such use and there are, therefore, no individual campsites. However, campsites do exist outside the region of the park and are usually available. Information on campsites outside the park can be obtained by writing to: Ontario Travel, Queen's Park, Toronto, Ontario. M7A 2E5. Leamington, the nearest community to the park, offers hotel and motel accommodation, food, and other supplies.

For a better understanding and appreciation of the park's complex natural environment, you are urged to share in the interpretive programme which is conducted by a park naturalist and his staff. Throughout the year conducted hikes and special programmes are available. At the Interpretive Centre slide and film programmes are offered, as well as talks and displays depicting the park through every season. Information regarding these events are posted on the bulletin boards and at the information desk in the Interpretive Centre.

Just a few don'ts! Open fires are not allowed in the park. But you may bring your own barbecue or use those provided at picnic facilities. Please don't forget the people who will visit the park after you: use the receptacles provided and leave your picnic site clean.

Dogs and cats are welcome in the park, and you need no special permit or vaccination certificate. But dogs should be kept on a leash and under control at all times.

Finally, collecting or molesting any animal or plant is strictly forbidden within the park. Park officials are particularly alert to any infringement of this ruling.

The park is accessible by automobile from Leamington on Highway No. 3 and from Highway No. 18. Leamington may be reached by bus either from the east or west or from Windsor. Through air or train service is available to Windsor.

This, very briefly, is Point Pelee. Relax, share and enjoy it! This unique natural heritage is yours to marvel at. A visit to Point Pelee is an experience I'm sure you will wish to repeat again and again.

Further inquiries concerning Point Pelee National Park should be addressed to:

Superintendent,
Point Pelee National Park,
RR#1, Leamington, Ontario.
N8H 3V4

Checklist of Birds

Wood Thrush

CHECKLIST OF BIRDS

Three hundred and twenty-four species of birds and two hybrids have been recorded at Point Pelee from 1877 to May, 1977. In the following listing species that are assumed without proof to have been correctly identified and recorded are marked H, those that are very rare are marked VR and those that are accidental are marked ACC.

Loons
 Common Loon
 Arctic Loon H
 Red-throated Loon VR
Grebes
 Red-necked Grebe VR
 Horned Grebe
 Eared Grebe VR
 Western Grebe H
 Pied-billed Grebe
Pelicans, Gannets, Cormorants
 White Pelican VR
 Gannet ACC
 Double-crested Cormorant
Herons, Bitterns
 Great Blue Heron
 Green Heron
 Little Blue Heron VR
 Cattle Egret
 Great Egret
 Snowy Egret VR
 Black-crowned Night Heron
 Yellow-crowned Night Heron
 Least Bittern
 American Bittern
Ibises
 Glossy Ibis VR
 White Ibis ACC
Swans, Geese, Ducks
 Mute Swan VR
 Whistling Swan
 Canada Goose
 Brant H

 Snow Goose
 Mallard
 Black Duck
 Gadwall
 Pintail
 Green-winged Teal
 Blue-winged Teal
 Cinnamon Teal H
 European Wigeon VR
 American Wigeon
 Northern Shoveler
 Wood Duck
 Redhead
 Ring-necked Duck
 Canvasback
 Greater Scaup
 Lesser Scaup
 Common Goldeneye
 Barrow's Goldeneye ACC
 Bufflehead
 Oldsquaw
 Harlequin Duck VR
 King Eider VR
 White-winged Scoter
 Surf Scoter
 Black Scoter
 Ruddy Duck
 Hooded Merganser
 Common Merganser
 Red-breasted Merganser
Vultures, Hawks, Eagles
 Turkey Vulture
 Goshawk

Sharp-shinned Hawk
Cooper's Hawk
Red-tailed Hawk
Red-shouldered Hawk
Broad-winged Hawk
Swainson's Hawk H
Rough-legged Hawk
Golden Eagle
Bald Eagle
Marsh Hawk
Ospreys, Falcons
Osprey
Gyrfalcon H
Peregrine Falcon
Merlin
American Kestrel
Grouse, Quails, Pheasants
Ruffed Grouse VR
Bobwhite VR
Ring-necked Pheasant

Cranes
Sandhill Crane VR
Rails, Gallinules, Coots
King Rail
Virginia Rail
Sora
Yellow Rail VR
Common Gallinule
American Coot
Plovers, Turnstones
Semipalmated Plover
Piping Plover VR
Killdeer
American Golden Plover
Black-bellied Plover
Ruddy Turnstone
Woodcock, Snipe, Sandpipers
American Woodcock
Common Snipe
Whimbrel

Blue-grey Gnatcatcher

Bewick's Wren

Upland Sandpiper VR
Spotted Sandpiper
Solitary Sandpiper
Willet VR
Greater Yellowlegs
Lesser Yellowlegs
Red Knot
Purple Sandpiper VR
Pectoral Sandpiper
White-rumped Sandpiper
Baird's Sandpiper
Least Sandpiper
Dunlin
Short-billed Dowitcher
Long billed Dowitcher H
Stilt Sandpiper
Semipalmated Sandpiper
Western Sandpiper
Buff-breasted Sandpiper
Marbled Godwit VR
Hudsonian Godwit VR
Ruff VR
Sanderling
Avocets, Phalaropes
American Avocet VR
Red Phalarope VR
Wilson's Phalarope
Northern Phalarope
Jaegers, Gulls, Terns
Pomarine Jaeger VR
Parasitic Jaeger
Long-tailed Jaeger ACC
Glaucous Gull VR
Iceland Gull VR
Great Black-backed Gull
Herring Gull
Ring-billed Gull
Laughing Gull VR
Franklin's Gull
Bonaparte's Gull
Little Gull
Black-legged Kittiwake VR
Sabine's Gull H
Forster's Tern

Common Tern
Caspian Tern
Black Tern
Murres
  Thick-billed Murre ACC
Pigeons, Doves
  Rock Dove
  Mourning Dove
Cuckoos
  Yellow-billed Cuckoo
  Black-billed Cuckoo
Barn Owls, Typical Owls
  Barn Owl VR
  Screech Owl
  Great Horned Owl
  Snowy Owl VR
  Long-eared Owl
  Short-eared Owl
  Saw-whet Owl
Goatsuckers
  Chuck-will's widow VR
  Whip-poor-will
  Common Nighthawk
  Lesser Nighthawk ACC
Swifts, Hummingbirds
  Chimney Swift
  Ruby-throated Hummingbird
  Rufous Hummingbird ACC
Kingfishers
  Belted Kingfisher
Woodpeckers
  Common Flicker
  Pileated Woodpecker H
  Red-bellied Woodpecker VR
  Red-headed Woodpecker
  Yellow-bellied Sapsucker
  Hairy Woodpecker
  Downy Woodpecker
  Black-backed Three-toed VR
  Northern Three-toed VR
Flycatchers
  Eastern Kingbird

Western Kingbird VR
Great Crested Flycatcher
Eastern Phoebe
Yellow-bellied Flycatcher
Acadian Flycatcher
Willow Flycatcher
Alder Flycatcher
Least Flycatcher
Eastern Wood Pewee
Olive-sided Flycatcher
Larks, Swallows
  Horned Lark
  Tree Swallow
  Bank Swallow
  Rough-winged Swallow
  Barn Swallow
  Cliff Swallow
  Purple Martin
Jays, Magpies, Crows
  Gray Jay VR
  Blue Jay
  Black-billed Magpie VR
  Common Raven VR
  Common Crow
Titmice, Nuthatches, Creepers
  Black-capped Chickadee
  Boreal Chickadee VR
  Tufted Titmouse VR
  White-breasted Nuthatch
  Red-breasted Nuthatch
  Brown Creeper
Wrens
  House Wren
  Winter Wren
  Bewick's Wren VR
  Carolina Wren
  Long-billed Marsh Wren
  Short-billed Marsh Wren
Mockingbirds, Thrashers
  Mockingbird
  Gray Catbird
  Brown Thrasher

Sage Thrasher ACC
Thrushes, Bluebirds
American Robin
Wood Thrush
Hermit Thrush
Swainson's Thrush
Gray-cheeked Thrush
Veery
Eastern Bluebird
Mountain Bluebird ACC
Townsend's Solitaire ACC
Gnatcatchers, Kinglets
Blue-gray Gnatcatcher
Golden-crowned Kinglet
Ruby-crowned Kinglet
Pipits, Waxwings
Water Pipit
Bohemian Waxwing VR
Cedar Waxwing
Shrikes, Starlings
Northern Shrike
Loggerhead Shrike VR
Starling
Vireos
White-eyed Vireo
Bell's Vireo VR
Yellow-throated Vireo
Solitary Vireo
Red-eyed Vireo
Philadelphia Vireo
Warbling Vireo
Warblers
Black-and-white Warbler
Prothonotary Warbler
Worm-eating Warbler
Golden-winged Warbler
Brewster's Warbler (Hybrid)
Lawrence's Warbler (Hybrid)
Blue-winged Warbler
Tennessee Warbler
Orange-crowned Warbler
Nashville Warbler

Virginia's Warbler ACC
Northern Parula
Yellow Warbler
Magnolia Warbler
Cape May Warbler
Black-throated Blue Warbler
Yellow-rumped Warbler
Black-throated Gray Warbler H
Townsend's Warbler ACC
Black-throated Green Warbler
Cerulean Warbler
Blackburnian Warbler
Yellow-throated Warbler VR
Chestnut-sided Warbler
Bay-breasted Warbler
Blackpoll Warbler
Pine Warbler
Kirtland's Warbler VR
Prairie Warbler
Palm Warbler
Ovenbird
Northern Waterthrush
Louisiana Waterthrush
Kentucky Warbler
Connecticut Warbler
Mourning Warbler
Common Yellowthroat
Yellow-breasted Chat
Hooded Warbler
Wilson's Warbler
Canada Warbler
American Redstart
Weaver Finches
House Sparrow
Meadowlarks, Blackbirds, Orioles
Bobolink
Eastern Meadowlark
Western Meadowlark VR
Yellow-headed Blackbird VR
Red-winged Blackbird
Orchard Oriole
Northern Oriole

Rusty Blackbird
Brewer's Blackbird VR
Common Grackle
Brown-headed Cowbird
Tanagers
Scarlet Tanager
Summer Tanager
Grosbeaks, Finches,
Sparrows, Buntings
Cardinal
Rose-breasted Grosbeak
Blue Grosbeak VR
Indigo Bunting
Dickcissel VR
Evening Grosbeak
Purple Finch
Pine Grosbeak VR
Hoary Redpoll H
Common Redpoll
Pine Siskin
American Goldfinch
Red Crossbill VR
White-winged Crossbill VR
Rufous-sided Towhee

Lark Bunting ACC
Savannah Sparrow
Grasshopper Sparrow
LeConte's Sparrow VR
Henslow's Sparrow
Sharp-tailed Sparrow VR
Vesper Sparrow
Lark Sparrow ACC
Bachman's Sparrow VR
Cassin's Sparrow H
Dark-eyed Junco
Tree Sparrow
Chipping Sparrow
Clay-colored Sparrow
Field Sparrow
Harris' Sparrow VR
White-crowned Sparrow
White-throated Sparrow
Fox Sparrow
Lincoln's Sparrow
Swamp Sparrow
Song Sparrow
Lapland Longspur
Snow Bunting